BENSON

THE AUTOBIOGRAPHY

BY **George Benson**

with Alan Goldsher

Foreword by **BILL COSBY**

DA CAPO PRESS

A Member of the Perseus Books Group

Designed by George Whipple
Set in 11.3 point Minion Pro by Westchester Publishing Services

Cataloging-in-Publication data for this book is available from the Library of Congress.
ISBN: 978-0-306-82229-2
ISBN (e-book): 978-0-306-82230-8

Published by Da Capo Press
A Member of the Perseus Books Group
www.dacapopress.com

Da Capo Press books are available at special discounts for bulk purchases in the U.S. by corporations, institutions, and other organizations. For more information, please contact the Special Markets Department at the Perseus Books Group, 2300 Chestnut Street, Suite 200, Philadelphia, PA 19103, or call (800) 810-4145, ext. 5000, or e-mail special.markets@perseusbooks.com.

10 9 8 7 6 5 4 3 2 1

Contents

Foreword

In 1964 I was an up-and-comer who was becoming a *name*, and man, it was exciting. I'd made the climb from small coffeehouses, to not-quite-as-small folk music rooms, to nightclubs on the level of New York's Basin Street East and the Village Gate—rooms that sat 180-something people, rooms that had liquor licenses, rooms where comedians like Dick Gregory were the headliners. Sometimes I opened for singers and musical groups, and sometimes, they opened for me. One week I'd share the bill with the wonderful South African singer Miriam Makeba, and a few months later it would be the incredible tenor saxophonist Stan Getz. These weren't the kinds of joints that booked guys like Frank Sinatra and Sammy Davis Jr.—Frank and Sammy played big-money places, like the Copacabana. Basin Street and the Gate weren't *showbiz* nightclubs as much as they were *hip* nightclubs.

It seemed like whenever I played the Gate, I'd run into this wonderful black gentleman by the name of Jimmy Boyd. One night, after a show, Jimmy told me about this guy, a young cat named George Benson. "I'm tellin' ya, Bill," he said, "this guy can really play. Really play, Bill. Really, *really* play. He's doing a gig up in Harlem. Why don't you come and see him?"

I said, "Yeah. Oh. Okay." But I didn't go. So he asked me again and again and again, and I still didn't go. I was performing with established artists like Miriam and Stan, and besides, I wasn't yet in a position where I could help out this youngster of whom I'd never heard. I didn't *make* time to *do* time to *have* time. I had no excuses. Eventually, Jimmy gave up on me.

Over the next twenty years, for George Benson, the hits came. "This Masquerade." "Breezin.'" "On Broadway." "Love Ballad." "Give Me the Night." "Turn Your Love Around." One right after the other, right after the other. All you'd hear were people talking about George Benson, George Benson, George Benson. And almost every time I heard his name, I'd think about that wonderful, persistent Jimmy Boyd.

In 1987, I was asked to emcee the Playboy Jazz Festival at the Hollywood Bowl. George was the final act, and that was *huge* because he was following heavy hitters like Sarah Vaughan, Grover Washington Jr., Stan Getz, Joe Williams, Count Basie, Lionel Hampton, Branford Marsalis, and Etta James. (I wasn't surprised that George was the closer because, even eight years after its release, "On Broadway" was still killing the world.) The festival kicked off in the early afternoon, and the last act came on around ten thirty. We started in the light and would be finishing in the dark, so I knew that last act—well, he'd better be good, because if he wasn't, the people would *leave*. They were tired, man. They were worn out. They'd watched acts come and go, and come and go, and come and go, and they would pick up their ice chests, which had nothing but melted ice pooled at the bottom, and go home. If George wasn't good from note one, it might turn out to be Amateur Night at the Apollo, with all the booing and everything.

When it was time, I said, "Ladies and gentlemen, George . . ." and the place erupted. They never even heard me say "Benson." For all they knew, I was introducing George Washington or George Foreman. As I headed to the wings, I heard, *Brrrrump, brump. Ba-da-dum, da-dum. Brump, brump. Ba-da-dum, da-dum.* It was "On Broadway," and the people went even crazier. I watched every note of that show . . . and so did all 18,157 of the folks there. Nobody left. And George sang. And George played. And George, the showman, tore the place *up*.

Now we come to ten months ago. I'm at home, in Massachusetts, and in Massachusetts they have a channel on the television, channel 850, and it's progressive jazz. One night, I turn on this channel 850, then go into the bathroom to brush my teeth, and I hear a song:

"From This Moment On."

Blistering speed.

Bump-chicka-bump-d-d-d-bop-chicka-bop . . .

I grab the toothpaste.

Doo-doo-doo-deeeeee-b-b-b-bop-chicka-bowwww . . .

I put the toothpaste on the electric toothbrush.

B-b-b-b-bow-chicka-bop-bop-d-d-d-chicka-doo . . .

I put the electric toothbrush in my mouth and turn it on.

And then comes the guitar solo.

I turn off the electric toothbrush so I can hear the guitar solo.

And I've never heard a guitar solo like this. And I've heard the greats: Jim Hall. Charlie Byrd. Kenny Burrell. But this solo—*nothing like it*. This was a musician playing because he was a *musician*. This guy is burnin' up, but it's clear to me that he's not just playing fast to play fast—this guy has a brain and is capable of playing as fast as he thinks, and he is a fast thinker. I *know* this because I'm *listening*, man.

Wow is not the word, but "Wow" is what I shout. With the toothpaste in my mouth. And the toothpaste splatters all over the sink, and the spigot, and the mirror. And the solo keeps going, and I make the same face I made when I first tasted the mustard greens at Dooky Chase's Restaurant in New Orleans. At that moment, I'm happy to be on this earth.

By the time I run out of the bathroom to see who the guitarist is, the song is done, and I have no idea who was playing, and I'm *mad*. But then it hits me, and I make a wager with myself: *I bet it's George*

Benson. The next morning, I call my friend Darlene Chan, one of the producers of the Playboy Jazz Festival, and say, "The next time you talk to George, can you ask him if he ever recorded 'From This Moment On' at blistering speed?"

The word comes back from Darlene later that afternoon: "George told me to tell you that you have a fantastic ear, and the answer is yes."

I hang up the phone, sit down, and have what I would call a reverse-epiphany sadness. I think, *This is the George Benson that Jimmy Boyd was trying to get me to see*, and then I say aloud, "You sure weren't lying, Jimmy. God bless you."

Bill Cosby
April 2012

Introduction

I didn't know folks in South Africa listened to me until their local concert promoters begged my management team to schedule some shows down there. And they kept begging, and begging, and begging some more, and it went on for months. Now, I didn't have much interest in performing down there—there were plenty of gigs in the States and Europe to keep me busy—but they were so frantic that they sent a couple of emissaries to Los Angeles to convince me it would be worth everybody's while.

During our meeting at my manager's office, I asked, "Why, guys? Why did you come all the way up here for this? I don't get it."

One of the promoters looked me dead in the eye and, in that nasal South African twang, said, "George, right now, you are the biggest selling artist in our country."

I said, "Huh. Nobody told me that. That's some good information."

"Yes, well, congratulations. Now we would like you to play six shows at a resort called Sun City, located in the city of Bophuthatswana. Please look at these."

He pulled out a pile of photos of a modern-day castle, with hundreds of guest rooms, some opulent swimming pools, and perfectly manicured lawns. Man, it was a sight to behold. I said, "This all sounds and looks beautiful, but I don't know, I've got a lot going on here at home, what with this recording session and that gig, and . . ."

He then interrupted with an offer I couldn't refuse. Papers were signed, hands were shaken, and the ball was rolling.

Now, I wasn't a history major or a geography expert, so I didn't know South Africa was a country unto itself—I just thought it was the southern part of Africa. I also wasn't all that politically oriented, so it wasn't until about a week before we left that, for the first time, I heard the word *apartheid*. And then the floodgates opened.

First, I got a call from the head of publicity at my record label, Warner Bros. "George," she said, "you're not really going to South Africa, are you? Race relations down there are a nightmare. You'll be sending the wrong message. As a matter of fact, if you play there, your career will be over. *Over.*"

I told her, "Wait a minute: This gig's been booked for weeks, and we're leaving in a few days, and you're asking me this *now*? Man, I *never* cancel gigs. All six shows are already sold out. They hired a sixty-piece orchestra to back me up. We're going."

"You know what, George," she continued, "you should probably know that there won't be any black people at the shows."

"Why not?" I asked.

"The tickets are forty dollars. Most black people in South Africa don't make that much in a month."

"Is that true, or are you just saying that so I won't go? How can you know that for a fact?"

"Okay, I don't know that for a fact," she admitted. "That's just what I've heard."

"Listen, there are going to be plenty of black people there, and I'll tell you why: If you tell a black man he can't have something, that's the first thing he'll want. Like if you say, 'You can't have a white woman,' he's going out to get himself a white woman. If you tell him he can't drive a Cadillac, the next time you see him, he'll be behind the wheel of a Seville. And if you tell him, 'You can't have George Benson tickets,' he'll be sitting in the third row. Trust me on that."

A few minutes after I hung up with her, my keyboard player called. "Man, I don't think I'm gonna go to South Africa. I don't wanna go to South Africa. South Africa, no way."

I sighed and said, "Okay, man, you don't have to go. I'll find a replacement."

He was quiet for a second. I don't think he believed I'd bring in somebody else. Finally, he said, "So you're going?"

"Yeah, man. I'm bringing my wife and my little boy. We're gonna have a great time. Those people out there, they're gonna take care of us."

He was quiet for a second, then said, "I guess if you're cool with taking your family, it'll be okay."

After that, my bass player called, and then my drummer, and then another Warner Bros. executive, all of whom tried to convince me to pull the plug on the trip. Finally, I came up with the perfect retort: Whenever one of them said, "I don't want to go, and you shouldn't go either," I'd ask them, "Do you sell your records in South Africa?" When they said yes, I'd say, "Then what the heck are you telling me not to play there for? If you don't want to do business with them, then get your records out of their stores." That quieted them down *quick*.

Our plane touched down in South Africa at about 2:00 a.m. local time, and there were hundreds of people at the gate, waiting to greet me. Before I could even voice my appreciation to the crowd, out of the corner of my eye, I saw a young black man running toward me, followed by four white police officers. I thought, *No, don't come this way. I can't have police attacking this kid. Heck, I can't have the police attacking me.*

The young black man came to a halt directly in front of me and wrapped his arms around my chest in what I guessed was a desperate attempt to avoid a beating. He said, "Mr. Benson, help! Please! Help! Don't let go of me! They won't hurt me if I'm with you!" I held on to this boy tight, because I knew in my heart and gut that he was right—if I let go of him, those officers would take him out behind the meta-phorical shack and kill him. Once they realized I wasn't releasing the kid, the officers stopped the chase, then, after a loud discussion filled with curse words, wandered away. When he was sure the police-men were gone, the man let go of me and said, "Welcome home, brother. Welcome home."

The next day, the promoters held a press conference in the hotel's ballroom, and the place was filled wall-to-wall with reporters and photographers—all of whom were white. After fifteen minutes of non-stop questions, a black man standing off to the side by himself raised his hand. I couldn't make out exactly what he said, but it sounded like, "Mr. Benson, as a black man, why are you here?"

After a stunned moment of silence, three policemen strode toward the reporter and made as if to remove him from the room. I said, "Hold up, leave that man alone! He has the right to ask me something." I then asked the reporter to repeat his question.

"As a black man, why are you here?" he said.

"First off, I'm a musician," I said, "not a politician. I was hired to play some music for your people, and that's what I'm going to do. Second of all, I call myself a Christian, so I have heard that it's been said love your neighbor and hate your enemy. However, I say to you, 'Love your friends, and pray for those who persecute you.'"

The next morning, that little quote of mine was on the front page of every newspaper.

From the get-go, it was obvious even to me that Sun City wasn't representative of South Africa in that it was far more progressive. A cross between Las Vegas and Disneyworld (except smaller), Sun City had a snowless ski resort, a pictorial safari, glitzy casinos, multiple state-of-the-art concert venues and discos, and—most importantly—a relatively positive vibe. You see, Sun City was one of the first places in the country where black people and white people could party together. And that was by design.

Sol Kerzner, the mastermind behind the resort, somehow convinced the South African government to allow Bophuthatswana enough autonomy to appoint its own president, a black man named Lucas Mangope. President Mangope, it turned out, was a huge jazz fan, and he and his wife came to each of my shows; they sat front row center, and were treated to what everybody agreed were six wonderful evenings of music.

The record company girl was wrong: The crowds at the shows were 50 percent white and 50 percent black, but this isn't to say we weren't touched by the country's innate racism and turmoil. The powers that be were so concerned for my safety that I was assigned a couple of machine-gun-wielding bodyguards, who followed me everywhere I went during the day and stood outside my hotel-room door every night. And the all-white orchestra from Johannesburg wanted nothing to do with our mostly black band, to the point that they wouldn't speak to us—the whole week, not a single word. But after those six wonderful shows, those orchestral cats finally came around. Before the final gig, each one of them tiptoed into my dressing room, one at a time, to thank me for the opportunity. I could tell it was a labor for them to say something kind to a black man, because they'd grown up under a different set of rules. They were taught that blacks were second-, third-, and fourth-class citizens who should be treated as such. But music, as is often the case, transcended racism and so shed a lifetime of racist teaching. In the moment, I had mixed emotions, but later on, I realized that what they'd done required a ton of courage on their part: the courage to *change*.

At the last minute, Sol booked us a gig in Cape Town for my last night in the country, and that was a big deal, a *huge* deal, because that city had never—*never*—hosted an interracial concert. My manager wasn't concerned for our safety—there was too much light shining on us for something to go down. His primary concern was that all the black concertgoers would be stuck in the back while the white folks sat up front.

"George," he said, "I don't want the only faces you see to be white ones, so we're doing this my way. Here's what's gonna happen: We're selling tickets in groups of four. So a group of four whites might be by a group of four blacks, whether they like it or not. Nobody will know where they're sitting. The only thing they're guaranteed is that they'll sit with someone in their party."

And it worked. That night, the front row was white-white-white-white-black-black-black-black-white-white-black-black-white-black-white-black. Same with the second row. And the third. And so on. It was beautiful.

Except for the riot squads.

Certain there were going to be fights, the government had policemen in riot gear all up and down the sides of the hall. They were armed with guns and tear gas, wearing flak jackets and helmets, looking like they were ready to go to war. All for a jazz concert. As I counted off our opening tune, I looked at those heavily armed officers and wondered what my first long-term music employer, a salty organist by the name of Brother Jack McDuff, would think about the whole thing. Knowing McDuff, he'd probably pull out a switchblade and threaten to mess some people up, then he'd take a puff of some reefer.

Near the end of the show—which, from where we were standing, felt like it was exceptionally well received—I launched into "The Greatest Love of All"—a tune I'd recorded for a Muhammad Ali biopic, a tune that took my career to the moon—and almost immediately after the first bar, a couple of folks in the front row held up a lit candle. A couple more people followed suit. And then a dozen more. And then a hundred more. And then a thousand more. Soon, almost every one of the 8,510 people in the house was waving a candle. And locking arms. And swaying side to side.

Black and white alike.

The candles had lit up the hall to the point that I could see virtually everybody's face, and many of those faces were covered with tears. I'd only seen something like that once before, at a Mahalia Jackson Easter Sunday gig I played back in 1967—that wasn't a surprise, though, because Mahalia Jackson could make *anybody* cry—but this went beyond even that. This was about togetherness, and new beginnings, and love for your fellow man.

Little surprise that when I turned around, my entire band was in tears. At that moment, for the first and only time in my music-playing life, I almost broke down onstage. But I somehow managed to keep it together and finish the song. I had to, really, because those people deserved it. The next morning, I left South Africa a better man than I'd been when I'd arrived.

Fast-forward twenty-three years. I'd just finished a show in South Africa, and a familiar-looking young man wandered over and said, "Hi, George. You probably don't remember me, but I was part of the production team at that show in Cape Town."

I snapped my fingers and said, "I *do* remember you! You used to hang out with my bodyguards!"

"That's right! But . . ." He looked over his shoulder, as if to make certain nobody was listening to us, then leaned close to me and whispered, "Those weren't your bodyguards."

"What do you mean?" I whispered back.

"If a riot broke out, those men were going to assassinate you, and it would be told that you got killed in the fray. That way, South Africa would never have another interracial concert again."

Speechless, I stared at this earnest young man and thought, *Man, how the heck did a kid from Pittsburgh almost get himself assassinated in the middle of South Africa?*

1 The Steel City

The Pittsburgh of the first half of the twentieth century had a bad rap, man, as much for what it *wasn't* as for what it *was*, as much for what it *didn't* have as for what it *did*. There weren't any cultural upheavals in Pittsburgh, no Harlem Renaissances or Jazz Ages or any of that business. The city had steel mills, ghettos, dirt, segregation, and racism. Folks went to work, then they came home, then they did it again and again and again—but that's not a bad thing. That's what most Americans did then, and it's what most Americans do now. They go to their job, they try to do it better than anybody else, they get their paycheck, they take care of their family as best they can, they hopefully listen to some music, and they live a good life.

But Pittsburgh wasn't *all* mundane, gritty, and pedestrian; the city did produce its fair share of jazz cats. Art Blakey, one of the baddest drummers in bebop history—and one of the nicest guys you'll ever meet—was born and bred in Pittsburgh. Erroll Garner, as pretty a piano player as you'll hear, was also a Pittsburgh boy. Ray Brown—who was to bass what Art Blakey was to drums—was another one, as was the piano player Horace Parlan; the sweet trombonist Slide Hampton (Slide was actually from nearby Jeannette, but we'll claim him as our own); and the brilliant, brilliant piano man Earl "Fatha" Hines (Earl was born in Duquesne, but we'll take him, too). And then there was J. C. Moses, who *killed* on drums alongside everybody from bebopping Bud Powell to sax screamer Eric Dolphy; Bob Babbitt, who thumped the bass on all those Motown Records hits; the great, great, great, great Ahmad Jamal, whose piano was a direct influence on Miles Davis's trumpet; Dakota Staton, who could jazz up the blues and blues up the jazz like few other girl singers; Roy Eldridge, whose nickname was Little Jazz but could've been Bigger Than Big Jazz because of that fat tone of his; Beaver Harris, a fine drummer who wanted to be Max Roach when he grew up; and Eddie Jefferson, the greatest scatter in the history of bebop. Oh, and let's not leave out composer/bandleader Henry Mancini, composer/arranger Billy Strayhorn, and bassist/genius Paul Chambers.

And of course we can't forget yours truly, George Washington Benson, a Pittsburgh jazz cat through and through.

My grandfather was a businessman named Major Evans, a hard worker and an ideas guy, always doing something to create a livelihood for himself. His favorite hobby was to squat down, take a deep breath, and pick up the back end of a Model T Ford; that's how he demonstrated his physical prowess, what he used to call "my strength." Years later, when I was old enough to know better, I got a chance to hang out with him, to find out what kind of guy he was and, most importantly, to see that he and I shared a lot of traits. I never lifted up the back of a car, but we were both headstrong, and we both liked to perform. Anybody with two eyes and two ears could tell within two minutes that we were from the same bloodline.

I was born in 1943—March 22, to be exact. My mother, Erma, had just turned fifteen, and my birth father, Charles Evans, was off fighting for America in World War II—I didn't see the man until I was four years old. Heck, I guess I was two before he even knew he had a kid. But, man, he was just a kid himself, maybe nineteen, married to a young French girl.

Charles Evans found out about George Washington Benson when he was still stationed overseas, but he didn't hear about me from my mother. The story goes that he was in a foxhole, ducking bullets—

and firing back a few of his own—when one of his buddies came over and said, "Man, that boy looks just like you!"

My dad said, "What boy are you talking about?" The only boys Charles was concerned about right at that minute were the boys who were pointing guns at his head.

"That boy back home," his buddy said. "Yeah, you got a son, man. He looks *just* like you."

I finally met my dad when I was four. He was a tall man . . . or at least he seemed tall, especially when he put me on his shoulders and I saw Pittsburgh from one heck of a different angle. He was a stocky guy, small but lots of muscles, a live wire. And I bet if the circumstances were right, he could've lifted up a Model T, just like his daddy.

I lived with my mother in an impoverished neighborhood of Pittsburgh, but you know what? We didn't know what poor meant. We just lived our lives, and it was a good life, and being in the ghetto didn't matter one bit. I ate every day. My mother treated me kindly—heck, everyone around me in our neighborhood was kind. There was no poor. There was no rich. There was just *life*.

We lived in a hotel located right off of a place called Gilmore Alley, right in the heart of the ghetto of Pittsburgh . . . and Gilmore Alley was an actual alley, with dirty brick walls, garbage cans, and rodents. But it never bothered me. When you're a kid, you take what's given to you, and you don't complain . . . at least maybe until later.

Mother was a church person, and she was always looking for the answers to life's questions in the Bible. There were a lot of churches in our neighborhood, and I saw all of them: the ones that were beautiful and hosted wealthy parishioners, the ones that were crumbling and falling to pieces, and the ones that weren't even churches—they were temporary tents. On a rainy, muddy Sunday when I was five or so, we went to a tent church. As the parishioners sang, the preacher jumped up and down, and made all kinds of funny noises. Something about it upset me, so I cried. My mother said, "If you start crying, I'm not going to buy you no sundae." The ice cream sundae at the drugstore was my reward for not making any noise at church—and, man, I always looked forward to those sundaes. My crying ended just like that.

Not only was Mother a spiritual-minded person, but she always sang, so much so that her nickname in high school was Sing. She even hummed little melodies when she was nursing me, and all those songs stayed in my head. That's probably how I got my start in music. (Then again, music might've been in my blood, as my father played trombone, drums, and piano. He wasn't a professional, but word on the street was that Charles Evans was most definitely not a slouch.)

Going to church had one definite advantage: If you were a churchgoer and you wanted to sing, you sang—and, not only that, you sang in public. During holiday time, they took us downtown to a great department store, and I'd never been anywhere like it. It was bright and clean, and the Christmas shoppers walked up and down the aisles with pep in their step and gifts in their arms, a sight that left me longing for that life . . . but just a little bit. The sound of the choir bounced off of all the walls, then right back into our ears, and I thought, *This is exciting. This is big time.* But since my mother changed churches as often as some folks change their socks, singing in a store was a rare opportunity.

I went to Letsche Elementary School, an integrated but mostly African American school, located, ironically, right next door to the school I went to later, Connelly Vocational High School—and I say "ironically" because few African Americans could get into Connelly. You really had to have tremendous grades, a track record of good behavior, and some obvious potential. Once the music teachers at Letsche found out I could sing, that was it; they called me up for everything. "All right, Little Georgie," they'd say, "come on up here and sing something for us." (Most folks called me Little Georgie, because I was smaller than most of the other boys in my class.) Thanks to the singing, yours truly, Little Georgie Benson, became popular around the school. As I've always found, music can open the lines of communication between old people and young, between black people and white.

I also tried to play a few instruments, one of which was the old, raggedy piano in the living room of our hotel. The piano didn't grab me much because it was beat up to the point of unplayability, plus my hands were too small to do much with the keys. It was fun banging around for a little bit every once in a while, but it got old fast. (I'm sure my mother wasn't particularly disappointed that I stopped beating the heck out of that raggedy keyboard.) Next came the violin, and that stuck because it was manageable: a lightweight, easy-to-carry instrument with four strings and a thin neck I could handle. It wasn't the coolest axe in the world, but that didn't faze me, because if I heard a tune off of the radio, I could more or less play it by ear—I didn't need to read music, so I didn't learn how to read music—and the ability to entertain my mother with a song mitigated the instrument's alleged uncoolness.

Gilmore Alley was right by Fullerton Street, one of the friendliest, most vibrant blocks in our immediate area. There was always hustle, always bustle, and always shouts of "Got any I? Anybody want any I today?" I referred to ice. These guys were ice farmers. Ice was the only thing you could farm in our neighborhood—they didn't have any cows, goats, or chickens in the ghetto. But why was ice such an important commodity, you might ask? Well, there were no refrigerators in Gilmore Alley because we didn't have any electricity. For us, the icebox in the kitchen kept our food fresh, and the gas lamps on the wall kept the room bright.

In the summer they'd holler, "I . . . I . . . I . . ."; conversely, when it got cold you'd hear, "Coal man, coal man, coal man!" (See, coal was even more important than ice, because it was easier to find ways to stay cool in the summer than it was to stay warm in the winter. If you're freezing cold in January, well, there're only so many layers you can put on. In Gilmore Alley, coal was a basic necessity, right up there with food, water, clothing, shelter, and music.) One day, one of the coal men dumped a huge pile of the black rocks right at the entrance to our alley, and for us kids, man, that was an invitation to climb. I ran up the mound, then back down, then up, then down. During my next trip to the top, a car sped around the corner—a '42 Chevy, to be precise—and came to a sudden, loud stop. The driver stepped out of the car, and he was wearing what we called an apple hat, the same kind made famous by Charlie Christian—or at least famous among in-the-know jazz fans. (Charlie, for those of you not in the know, wasn't just one of the first bebop guitar players in history, but one of the first beboppers *period*. What he was doing alongside clarinetist Benny Goodman in 1939 was so advanced that even today, it sounds relevant to the point of innovation. If you're a guitar player and you don't know Charlie Christian up, down, and sideways, you'd better start doing your homework because there'll be a test on this material next time I'm in your town.) The cat with the hat came over to the coal pile and called up to me, "Hey little boy! Can you tell me where Erma Benson lives?"

"You mean my mother? Yeah, she lives right here," I said, pointing to our house.

"No, I'm not looking for your mother," he said. "I'm looking for Erma Benson."

I said, "Yeah, yeah, she's right here." He seemed like a good guy, so I jumped down off of the coal pile and led him to our place. And that's how Tom Collier, the man who would one day become my stepfather, found out that Erma Benson, the object of his desire, had a child.

Tom was a novice guitar player—he was probably self-taught—but what he lacked in knowledge he made up for in passion and enthusiasm. I mean, man, he *loved* the instrument, *loved* jazz, and *really* loved Charlie Christian . . . which, of course, explained the hat. And that cat was protective of his axe. On the first day we moved into the Benson Hotel on Bedford Avenue, a three-story building with three other families, he put his acoustic guitar on a chair, knelt down, pointed at it, looked me straight in the eye, and said, "Now whatever you do, George, don't touch that guitar."

"Okay."

"I mean it."

"Okay."

"Now I have to go to the bathroom. Promise you won't touch it?"

"I promise."

The second he left the room, I ran over, picked up the guitar, and started strumming, *ding, dong, ding, dong, plink, plunk, plink, plunk.* Because what seven-year-old does what they're told?

Considering the speed and intensity with which he ran out of the bathroom, I was sure I was going to get a whupping, but he just gave me a smile, shook his head, and said, "Now you're going to have to learn how to play it. If you're going to be touching my guitar, you're going to have to learn how to play it."

Cool!

My hands were definitely too small for the guitar, so Tom took to the street and found a ukulele in a garbage can. No surprise, it was all cracked to pieces, as if somebody had purposely trashed it. (Why anybody would harm an instrument of any kind is beyond me.) But Tom was a handyman, and he got right to work—a little bit of glue, a set of strings, some ingenuity, and just like that, I had my first axe.

Tom taught me to play a few chords, but I took it from there, and being that it had four strings just like my violin, it wasn't as difficult as it would've been had I not already been a plucker and a sawer. Another reason I took to the uke so quickly: my ears. I still couldn't read music, but I was a great listener—you could attribute that to the fact that my mother sang to me all the time—and with some work, my fingers were almost always able to figure out what to do. I wasn't trying to play anything particularly complex, mind you—just a few ditties from movie sound tracks by people like Jo Stafford and Virginia

Mayo. Sometimes I was successful, and sometimes I wasn't, but it was always a blast.

Tom had a record player, too—a portable . . . or at least it was *called* a portable. He played me a whole lot of Charlie Christian's recordings with the Benny Goodman Sextet—little did anybody know that I'd someday share the stage and the studio with Benny himself; more about that later—and some records by George Shearing, the brilliant blind pianist whose star was rising beyond the moon.

Right next to the record player, there was a box. Plugged into the box, there was what I called a wire. And that wire was plugged into a guitar. Now, I'd never seen a guitar into which you could plug stuff. The first time I saw Tom click it on, I thought, *What's this going to do?* I mean, I'd never seen *anything* plugged into a guitar, *ever*. Tom picked up the axe, gave it a strum, and *Brrrrrmmmmggggggggg*, there was the Sound, and I couldn't believe it. I didn't just hear that guitar—I *felt* it in my bones, my muscles, and my heart. Fascinated, I sat on the floor with my back against the speaker and listened to the Sound for hours. I was hooked on electric guitar from the very beginning.

Discovering electric guitar was important, of course, but equally important to me—and this may sound funny, but it's true—was Pittsburgh's newspaper-selling program, a program that kids were allowed to join when they were seven. (Can you imagine that today? Seven-year-olds selling papers? Or seven-year-olds selling anything other than lemonade out in front of their houses? Me, neither.) Wanting to help out around the house, I hopped aboard, and soon enough, I was among the best of the best. One evening, I was sitting on the steps in front of the hotel, entertaining my girlfriends with my ukelele, keeping my eye on the big clock on top of one of the nearby buildings, knowing that if I didn't pick up my papers at the nearby newsstand by seven, I wouldn't have anything to sell that evening. I got so wrapped up in my performance that I lost track of the time; the next time I looked up, it was 6:59, which meant I had only one minute to run the three blocks and procure my papers. I stopped singing and told the girls, "Oh, I've got to go," then sprinted down to the newspaper stand, careful not to trip and fall, and bust my ukelele.

The newspaper stand was on Wylie Avenue and Fulton Street, right in the heart of the action, right across the street from the Stanley's Bar and Grille—the bar where everybody who was anybody in the jazz world played: Charlie Parker, Billy Eckstine, Art Blakey, *everybody*. The man at the stand gave me my five newspapers for the evening, which I would (hopefully) sell for a nickel apiece, which would earn me a penny and a half per paper. (When you run the numbers, you'll dig that if you sold all five of your papers, you'd get seven and a half cents. But they don't make half cents, so they'd round it down to seven. Not up to eight. Down to seven. That's Pittsburgh math for you.)

My first stop was a bar called Spokane's, and man, that was a rough place to sell papers—heck, it was a rough place to sell *anything*, what with all the people making all kinds of racket, and the jukebox blaring tunes of all shapes and sizes, plus the smoke was so thick that I could barely see a foot in front of me. I'd walk through the place, tap somebody on the knee, give them my most charming look, and say, "Excuse me, mister, would you like to buy a paper?" Most of the time, nobody even knew I was there—I was a little boy, after all, and that place was *noisy*.

I had less than one hour to move some merchandise, because my mother wanted me home at eight, so since nothing was happening at Spokane's, I took it to the street. As hard as it was to move any merchandise inside the bar, it was that much harder outside, because most everybody was rushing home from work. (That taught me to always show up on time. Punctuality makes your life much easier and much better.) After a few minutes of nothing, I made my way back to the stand, but a man stopped me: "Hey, little boy, give me a newspaper."

"Oh. Oh! *Oh!* Oooooookay! That'll be five cents."

The guy reached into his pocket and pulled out a quarter. "This is all I've got," he said. "I don't have any other change."

My shoulders slumped. I'd lost the sale. But the gentleman took pity on me; he handed me the quarter and said, "Here. You keep the change."

"Really?" I asked.

"Really." I gave him his paper, he gave me my quarter, and we went our respective ways. I walked—no, strutted—to the newspaper stand, knowing that I'd cleared about twenty cents.

That money was burning a hole in my pocket, so I walked over to Goode's Drug Store, which had, as far as I was concerned, the best candy selection in the area. I peeked over the top of the candy counter—and that's as far as I was able to peek; it was exactly my height—and tried to figure out how to distribute my newfound wealth. A chocolate bar, maybe? Or some hard candies? A little of each? These were some difficult decisions, man.

Right as I was about to make my selection, a man tapped me on the shoulder and said, "Hey, boy. Can you play that thing?"

Without even thinking, I started strumming, then sang, "I used to spend my money to make you look real sweet / I wanted to be proud of you when we walk down the street / Now don't ask me to dress you up in satin and silk / Your eyes look like two cherries in a glass of buttermilk."

A crowd formed around me, probably shocked that a seven-year-old kid was singing "Bloodshot Eyes" by Wynonie Harris. When I got to the chorus, folks started reaching into their pockets and pulling out their spare change. As I tried to figure out how I was going to round up these tips, a boy pushed his way through the crowd: my cousin, Reginald Benson. Reginald, who was a year older than me, was a quick thinker, so he took off his baseball cap, held it out, and one by one, folks gave us their pennies, nickels, dimes, and quarters, *plink, plink, plink*. I took in three dollars, an outrageous amount of money for a single song. I gave Reginald seventy-five cents for his trouble, one quarter out of each dollar. Just like that, Reginald and I were *rich*.

Word started getting around. Folks learned who I was and what I did, and most everywhere I went, I'd get requests. There was a playground right down the street from Spokane's, a brand-new playground, probably the nicest around. One afternoon, after a few hours of playing, I was on my way back home, and I ran into two guys, one of whom I knew well: Mr. Nesbitt, the director at the local rec center where I shot pool, played basketball, and knocked around some Ping-Pong balls. Mr. Nesbitt said to his friend, "There he is. There's that kid right there. Little Georgie Benson. The one I was telling you about." He reached into his pocket and pulled out a coin. "Georgie, here's a quarter. Sing that song 'I Got the Blues.'"

"I Got the Blues" was one of my favorites, a tune by the great bebop singer Eddie Jefferson. At that point, I didn't know much about Eddie or his music, but I knew I liked his voice, and I knew I loved that song. (Heck, I love Eddie so much that I recorded his tune "Moody's Mood for Love" on multiple occasions, and it has remained a regular part of my set list ever since.)

Who was I to refuse a request, especially when it was accompanied by a quarter, so I belted out, "*I got the blues. I don't know how to lose it. I got the blues.*" I used to sing it twice as fast as I do now, so it probably didn't sound as bluesy as it should have. When I got to the second chorus, Mr. Nesbitt and his friend started laughing. I wondered, *What're they laughing at? What's wrong with these guys?* But I kept right on singing. The more I sang, the more they laughed, and it got to the point where they were literally rolling around on the ground, holding their stomachs, unable to catch their breath. I cut the song short, put the quarter in my pocket, and went on home.

Fast forward twenty-some-odd years. I was playing at a small club, and there he is, the man himself, Eddie Jefferson. He introduced himself—which was unnecessary, because once you saw Eddie Jefferson's weathered, smiling face, you'd recognize him anywhere.

After some pleasantries, he said, "George, you won't remember this, but when you were a little kid, I came to you on the street corner. You were singing 'I Got the Blues' . . ."

I interrupted him: "Eddie, don't tell me that was you."

He grinned. "There's no way you remember that."

"Man, I *absolutely* remember that. It was you and another guy named Nesbitt."

"Holy moly, you *do* remember that!" he said.

"Like yesterday. And you just helped me over a hump. I was wondering why you guys were laughing so hard. Now I know why you were cracking up." We talked about that for what seemed like hours, and we had a ball. (Eddie was, unequivocally, the baddest bebop singer of all time. Nobody could touch him. It's like he was born to do just that: sing bop. One night at a club in Detroit I tried to compete with him, to scat against him like I was Billy the Kid, and it was no contest: The cat cut me into eighty-five different pieces.)

What with all this singing and getting paid, I knew I was onto something, so whenever we could, Reginald and I wandered up and down the street and stopped into any store that was still open. I'd play a tune, Reginald would pass the hat, and our fortune would grow and grow and grow. One evening on our way home, we came across a street fair, and that place was *jumping*—we're talking a Ferris wheel, cotton candy, popcorn, and shooting games. That night, believe me, we made great use of our hatful of money.

The money was flowing, but I was too young to open a bank account, so I did the next best thing: stored my money under my pillow. One morning I overslept, and my mother, wanting to make certain I didn't miss school, came into my bedroom and tapped me awake. I rolled over, and there was a plinking sound from my pillow. "What's that?" my mother asked.

"Um, nothing."

"That's not nothing," she said, then reached under my pillow and pulled out a handful of coins. Then another. Then another. "You're doing pretty good selling those papers, aren't you?" There was more money on my bed than she made in two weeks—she pulled in forty dollars every fourteen days, and I was making that each evening. But I didn't keep it all for myself—I gave most of it to my friends, a quarter here, fifty cents there. As long as I had enough to get a couple of candy bars, I was cool.

That night, while I was making some noise on one of my preferred street corners, a man wandered over and asked my name.

"Little Georgie Benson," I answered. Since all the little girls had now taken to calling me Little Georgie, I'd decided that would be my professional name.

He said, "Little Georgie, can you take me to your house and introduce me to your parents?"

That was one strange request. "Why?"

"Well, my name is Cephus Ford. I own a nightclub called Little Paris, and I'd like you to play there."

That ended the evening's concert. "Let's go."

When we got home, Cephus made his pitch. Mom stared at him silently for a bit, then said, "No. No, he can't."

Cephus looked as if somebody punched him in the gut. "Why not?" he asked.

"He's just a kid," Mom said, "and he's got to go to school."

"Not on weekends," Cephus pointed out. "If he worked Fridays and Saturdays, he wouldn't have any problems with being too tired to go to school the next day."

"But he's still too young."

He gave her an appraising look, then said, "I'll pay him forty dollars a night." Before she could answer, he said, "He'll go on at midnight, but I promise to have him home by one o'clock."

Mom agreed, and just like that, I was a professional musician, with a manager and everything. Granted, my manager was my soon-to-be stepfather Tom, but it was a start.

Little Paris was something else. That club was the first place I ever heard a live band, with drums and everything. But Cephus was about more than music: He wanted his patrons to have a *show*, and what a show they got, complete with stage girls who danced and kicked in unison, just like the Radio City Rockettes. The music was jazzy and funky, and everybody always had a good time.

I became a fixture. Sometimes I performed all by myself—singing, playing the ukelele, and dancing the night away—while other times Tom accompanied me on guitar. We must've been doing something right, because each set, without fail, the patrons threw money onto the stage. Those nights were the highlights of my week, month, and year.

One night, a few weeks into my tenure, the club's front doors flew open, and in came a dozen or so cops, all wielding hatchets and sledgehammers, and they chopped that place up, boy. They hammered the tables, the chairs, and the bar, as well as all of the liquor—booze and wood flew everywhere. When the dust settled, one of the cops pointed at me and said, "What's this little boy doing in here?"

Tom said, "That's my son! I'll get him right out of here." We grabbed my ukelele, stepped carefully over the broken tables, and headed to the door.

Another one of the cops said, "That's not his son, man! That's not his son!" It turned out that the officer knew my birth father. "Stop them! Hold them!"

So they stopped us and held us in the police station . . . alongside the house band and all the dancers.

The police station was a madhouse, with cops and prisoners yelling like crazy. They had all the men stay upstairs, and they brought Tom and me downstairs with the women. Soon after we got downstairs, one of the cops hollered to his buddies on the top floor, "Do you have any room for any women up there?" then he and the rest of the policemen started laughing.

Before I could ask Tom what was so funny, one of the cops snatched off one of the women's tops. When the bra came off, a couple of red balls fell to the ground, where they bounced against the wall. Tom covered my eyes immediately and said, "Don't even try to understand it, boy. Don't even look."

I learned later that these women were men, and those balls were make-believe breasts. Man, that was traumatic.

The judge who heard the case, he wasn't standing for any of this mess, but in retrospect, it makes perfect sense. A little boy in a dive of a nightclub, after midnight, surrounded by the riffraffiest of riffraff? Not good. They threatened to take me from my parents, then locked up Tom for six months.

When Tom got out of jail, the first thing he did was marry my mother, after which they made me some brothers and sisters, five to be exact. He asked my mother if I could continue my music career, and she said, "No. That's the end of that. No. He will do nothing. He already has a police record."

But none of that stopped me from making music. I took part in my school's music training course, headed up by Mr. Peeler and Miss Pugh. They were both nice people, Peeler and Pugh, but they had rules, and when it came to music, rules didn't seem to matter to me, especially since I saw them scuffling with songs that I could learn to sing in two seconds. I was always ready to jump out of my seat and tell them, "It goes like this! Come on with this! Play it! Play it! Play it!"

Another difficult adjustment was accepting the fact that everybody had an equal part, something I wasn't used to because I'd always been the front man. Eventually, I was kicked out of class, in part because I couldn't read music since I'd always learned by ear, and in part because they didn't need a ukelele or guitar player.

The summer I turned nine, I set aside the uke and took up guitar full time. Once I had the instrument more or less under my fingers—which didn't take too long; it wasn't like I needed to play like Segovia—I went back to the street corners and busked for change. One afternoon, a man approached me and said, "You're Little Georgie Benson, right?"

"Yeah."

"I know the guy who owns that barbershop down on Centre Avenue and Fullerton Street. He wants to meet you."

"Me? Why me?"

"Something about you playing one of his guitars."

Centre and Fullerton wasn't too far away, so off we went. When we arrived at the shop, he introduced me to the barber, who said, "When I heard about you, I told my friend, 'Hey, man, bring me that Little Georgie Benson cat I've been hearing so much about. I bet he could play my guitar.' See, I can't play the thing worth a lick, but I sure love the instrument." He pointed to the corner, and there it was, leaning against the wall, a brand-new Gibson L-5. I didn't know a thing about the makes and models of guitars, but I could tell that that one was special. (You know who else thought it was special? Wes Montgomery. For the majority of his brilliant career, that was his axe of choice.) "So go ahead, boy," the barber said. "Play that guitar."

I didn't have an electric guitar, just a little sixteen-dollar acoustic that I got for Christmas, and man, that thing was terrible on my hands: It gave me blisters, cuts, gouges, the works. So playing that fabulous Gibson, shiny and brand-new, that was a life-changing moment. It was like going from black and white to Technicolor, from two-dimensional to 3-D. The way it felt—smooth, light, and fast. The way that guitar sound got from the instrument, through the cord, and out the amplifier—*fascinating*! The way it sounded—warm, loud, and vibrant. It was like coming home. Strumming that impressive Gibson guitar through the equally impressive Gibson amp was a beautiful experience on every level, and I didn't want it to end. Fortunately, that afternoon—and for dozens of afternoons after—the barber let me play as long as I wanted to. Sometimes it was half an hour, sometimes it was forty-five minutes, and once in a while, it was even longer than that, but even if it was one minute, it was a true joy.

I took to it quickly, which on one hand was a surprise, because I hadn't spent any serious time on electric guitar; but on the other hand, it *wasn't* a surprise, because I believed with all my heart and soul that someday, I wouldn't have to play an instrument that tore my hands to shreds, that someday, I'd have an axe that would sing the same way I sang. And if you believe, you can make it happen.

A few weeks later, a man came into the barber shop, put his big, meaty hand on my shoulder, and said, "Little Georgie Benson, I know somebody who wants to meet you."

It seemed like there was always somebody who wanted to meet me, but I didn't mind. Oftentimes, it was fun being the center of attention. "Who's that?" I asked.

"His name is Harry Tepper. He owns the Sandwich Inn, that place up the street on Centre Avenue and Aaron Street."

I knew the Sandwich Inn—heck, everybody knew the Sandwich Inn, the home of the best pastrami sandwiches in Pittsburgh. But I'd never been there because my mother never let me go that far up Centre Avenue. I told the man, "I can't come."

"Why not? It's just a few blocks away."

"I have to get permission from my mother."

At this point, aside from getting arrested at Little Paris, I'd been an exemplary young man, so when I asked my mother about navigating the far end of Centre Avenue, she said, "Yeah, go ahead up. Just be careful."

The Sandwich Inn's counter was filled with more kinds of meat than I'd ever seen in my life, more kinds of meat than I even knew existed. The counter was low, so low that I could see over the top of it. A short man, maybe five feet six, with his back turned to me was hunched over the meat slicer, focusing all his concentration on making the perfect slice.

I said, "Excuse me, is Mr. Harry Tepper here?"

He turned around, gave me a once-over, and said, "You must be Little Georgie Benson."

"Yeah," I said, "that's me."

"Wait right there, man." He took off his apron, came around the counter, and shook my hand. "It's a pleasure to meet you. Listen, could you take me to your house and introduce me to your mother and father?"

"I suppose so. Why?"

He smiled. "It's a surprise. But I promise it'll make you happy."

Next thing I know, Harry Tepper, along with his partner Eugene Landy, are in our living room, talking to my mother and stepfather about taking me to New York and making a record.

2 Little Georgie Goes to New York

My parents didn't jump at Harry and Eugene's offer right away, and even at that age, I kind of understood why. I mean, here's a young sandwich guy from the rough side of town and his younger friend—Harry was twenty-two and Eugene was nineteen—who they've never met, strolling into their house and telling them they want to haul their ten-year-old kid up to New York and stick him in a recording studio. Anybody would question that. And while I understood, I didn't agree.

First of all, in my mind, Harry and Eugene weren't young at all—to me, if you were older than fifteen, you were a man, plus if a guy ran a sandwich place, he *had* to be a grown-up. Second of all, there weren't any child singers in Pittsburgh being hauled up to a New York recording studio, and why shouldn't I be the first? After what seemed like hours, Harry talked my mother into allowing Eugene to take me north and try to lock down a record deal. She agreed. He even convinced her to buy me a new guitar and a new lavender suit, complete with an oversized bow tie that went all the way out to my shoulders.

It bears mentioning that Eugene was slick, a handsome young fellow who, I found out later, was quite a hit with the ladies . . . lots and lots of ladies, as it turned out. One of his many girlfriends was a twenty-two-year-old schoolteacher who looked like Elizabeth Taylor.

Another was a well-off thirty-nine-year-old woman who managed the Bigelow Building, a fancy hotel not too far from my house. I remember him taking me up to her apartment—she was on the penthouse at the top, and you could see all of Pittsburgh from there. I'd never experienced anything like that in my life.

Eugene's wealthy thirty-nine-year-old girlfriend—let's say we call her Natalie—drove me, Harry, and Eugene up to New York in her 1955 Plymouth. (It turned out that Natalie was bankrolling our excursion, and it's fortunate she did, because it was one expensive trip.) She put us up at the Waldorf Astoria, which, at the time, was the most famous hotel in New York, maybe even the world. It was a beautiful room, probably the best they had, and the bill was $400 a night, which blew my mind. My family could've lived for a month on what she forked over for the hotel. She also took us to the Copacabana, and they let me in to the venerable nightclub, I'm guessing because she greased some palms.

When we hit town, the first thing I did was audition for *The George Jessel Show*, one of the few variety shows that had made the transition from radio to television. I didn't get picked and wasn't really told why. However, when I tried out for *The Arthur Godfrey Show* the next day, Arthur made it clear why he didn't want me: "I'm the only one here who plays ukelele." I wasn't even allowed the chance to sing a single note.

On the fourth morning, I was awakened by the sound of an argument from across the hall. (Think about that for a second: I could hear the yelling and hollering through two doors. That was one loud argument, man.) I poked my head out of the door and was treated to the sounds of Eugene and Natalie, hollering about this and that. After a few minutes, Eugene stormed out of the room and headed to the elevator, and if he saw me, he ignored me. Natalie followed him for a few steps, then, having noticed I was watching, turned around, put her hand on my shoulder, and gently led me back into the room and onto the bed. She knelt down and, with an earnest, caring look, said, "Little Georgie, you won't understand any of this, but Landy and I have had a falling out. I'm going back to Pittsburgh. Now, I want to say to you, if you decide to come back to Pittsburgh with me, I guarantee you that I'll get you that record deal that we're talking about. But if you say no, I'll understand. The decision is yours."

I didn't understand until that very moment how much I wanted to cut that record, how important it was for me to land that deal. Maybe it was because I wanted to help my family live a better life, maybe it was because I wanted to be famous, maybe it was because I wanted to give the world an opportunity to hear me make music, or maybe it was some combination of all of the above. But whatever the reason, the realization hit me like a pile of coal, and I burst into tears. "My mother expects me to come back with Landy because I left with him," I said—or at least I tried to say through all my crying. "So she expects me to come back with him. So I can't come back with you."

Natalie nodded. "I understand, George," she said, then gave me a warm hug and walked out of the room. I never saw her again. Landy and I went home the next day without ever setting foot in a recording studio. My career was at a standstill.

Fortunately, I only stood still for six months, at which point we flew up to New York, and I cut four sides for the RCA Victor label: "Shout, Holler and Scream," "A Little Boy's Dream," "She Makes Me Mad," and "It Shoulda Been Me." It wasn't until years later that I found out the guy who wrote the lyrics to "It Shoulda Been Me" was Curtis Ousley, a man you might know as King Curtis, a saxophonist who laid down some classic R&B instrumentals—"Yakety Yak," "Memphis Soul Stew," and "Ode to Billie Joe," just to name a few—and one of the few reed men who's been inducted into the Rock and Roll Hall of Fame.

I also laid down a version of "Mona Lisa," and I tried to do it like Nat King Cole—even then, I loved the man—and it sounded pretty good, but let's just say that there aren't too many prepubescent boys who can pull off an imitation of Nathaniel Adams Coles. (Once my voice changed, that was considerably less of an issue, and by the time 2011 rolled around, I figured I'd learned enough over the years that I could put together a credible tribute to the King, so we paid homage to the man during a show at Disney Hall in Los Angeles, an event I count as one of the proudest of my career. When we started the show, I told the audience, "There's something I want you to hear, in case you want to know how long I've been in love with Nat Cole." And then the crowd was treated to the sound of Little Georgie Benson singing "Mona Lisa," in a little high voice with the ukelele going *plink, plink, plink, plink, plink, plink.* When they realized it was me, the folks went crazy. Funnily enough, weeks before the show, the promoter asked me, "Who's going to sing Cole?" I told him, "Don't worry. We'll think of something.")

At that first session, I was backed by a band led by Leroy Kirkland, a composer, an arranger, and a guitarist who'd gigged or recorded with everybody from Erskine Hawkins to Screamin' Jay Hawkins, from Charlie Parker to the Dorsey Brothers, from Etta James to Ella Fitzgerald. Leroy was a pro's pro who'd been there and done that, and even though I was only ten, I could feel the gravity, experience, and creativity he brought to the studio surrounding him like a force field.

We finished up one of the tunes, and the guitar player, whose name was Carl Lynch, wandered off and left his axe resting on a stool. I picked it up and played some tune or another. A couple minutes later, Carl strolled over, smiled at me, and said, "Man, you're going to be a guitar player someday, an honest-to-goodness professional guitar player."

I smiled back. "Yeah? I'd like that," I said. "I like playing guitar."

He nodded, then repeated, "Well, you're going to be a guitar player. I can hear it."

(Fast-forward five years. I came to New York to cut a record with my doo-wop group, the Altairs. As was the case five years before, I spent the break messing around on one of the studio cats' guitars. A man came over and said, "You sing nice, but you're going to be a guitar player." I was so wrapped up in what I was doing that I gave him a polite thank you without even looking up. Fast-forward another four years, when I'd begun making a bit of noise as a guitarist. I was in yet another recording studio, and after our first tune, a man tapped me on the shoulder and said, "I know you. About five years ago you were on a session with this vocal group, and I told you that you were gonna be a guitar player."

And then it dawned on me. "Wait a minute, did you ever do a session with Leroy Kirkland?"

He snapped his fingers once, then said, "Man, you were just a kid. And I was right! You *are* a guitar player!" If I knew then what I know now, I wouldn't've been the least bit surprised. Carl Lynch was one of the heaviest studio cats on the New York scene for years and years, so he'd developed a darn good set of ears.)

The record, which was called *Little Georgie Benson: The Kid from Gilmore Alley*, was released on an RCA offshoot label called X. After it hit the street, I wasn't a little kid anymore; I was an eleven-year-old adult. I mean, how many kids had their agent run over to the local swimming pool and yell, "Get out of there and dry yourself off, Little Georgie! We have a radio interview to do!"

I'd tell Eugene, "But I'm playing with my friends!"

Then he'd yell in a voice I couldn't say no to, "Get out of there, man! We've only got twenty minutes! We've got to be on the radio!"

I was on the radio on a fairly regular basis—when it came to publicity, Eugene rarely said no—and my name also turned up in the newspaper every so often, so people in the neighborhood assumed I was rich. After all, the thinking went, if you heard somebody on the airwaves or read his name in print, he *must* be raking it in. And that made my mother nervous. She was always concerned that somebody would kidnap me and hold me ransom, then not believe her when she said she couldn't pay them to let me go.

The straw that broke the camel's back was when Eugene told my mother, "I'm going to take Little Georgie to Hollywood. I'm going to make a star out of him."

She said, "No. Unh-unh. No, you're not. You're not going to make a star out of my son. He's not going to Hollywood. He's not going *anywhere*."

And that was it. My career died before it was even given life. I was a has-been at eleven. It was all over. No Hollywood, no more recording studios, no more newspaper articles, no more trips to the Copacabana. I was just Little Georgie Benson, the kid who made a record but also got thrown out of music class.

So I went to school and lived like a normal kid, and realized pretty quickly that being a normal kid wasn't so bad. For that matter, it was good to have my life back, to hang out with my friends, to swim in the pool until I was ready to get out. It soon became apparent, however, that some things had changed. And those things, specifically, were the gangs.

In Pittsburgh, the major gangs, the scary gangs, the gangs that caused the most serious damage, were populated by men in their twenties. But there were also teen gangs, and if you were smart—if you didn't want to get in the middle of a possibly bloody recruiting war—you joined one. Actually, you didn't really have a choice. You *had* to join one, or you might get yourself beat up *bad*.

My cousin and I belonged to a gang that we kind of started ourselves, but it wasn't *really* a gang, because we didn't engage in ganglike activities. We just needed to be able to tell people we were in a gang. We were called the Junior Cavaliers, meaning we "belonged" to the Cavaliers. (Most of the gangs had a junior division, like the Jaguars had the Junior Jaguars, the Aces had the Junior Aces, and so on.) The Junior Cavaliers was just a couple of kids messing around, but it ended when one of my cousins was killed in a gang fight. When he got stabbed to death, well, that's when it stopped being some abstract thing and got very, very real.

And my cousin was the last guy I expected to get hurt, because he fought like Muhammad Ali in his prime: He was so fast and slick that no matter how hard you tried, you couldn't touch him. He made people furious because they'd be in a tussle with him and they would swing and miss, then my cousin would slide in one direction or the other and *bang*, it was over. And the whole time he'd be laughing, because fighting was so easy for him. In a way, it was probably enjoyable. One day he beat up this one cat so badly that the guy ran home and got his brothers, all of whom grabbed their guns and knives, and that was the end.

Even though I was done with the gangs, I managed to get myself into a fair amount of trouble. One afternoon, some friends and I were looking for a place to play basketball, and we ended up in a neighborhood that we shouldn't have ended up in, down by the high school on Fifth Avenue. (Trust me, if you lived in our neighborhood—known far and wide as "the Hill"—you wouldn't have wanted to be down by the high school on Fifth Avenue. The cats there hated anybody from the Hill, and if they found out that's where you lived, they'd run you right back up there.) But we didn't have anyplace else to play, and we weren't going to bother anybody, so we thought it would be okay.

It wasn't.

There were eight of us and twenty-five of them, and we didn't stand a chance. When I was about to dive in, I noticed one of my friends from school siding with our opponents, also getting ready to enter the fray. When he saw me, he backed off. He didn't want to rumble with me—for that matter, he didn't want to rumble at all if I was involved. Me, I had no choice.

Even though we were outnumbered like crazy, I thought we might be able to put up a good fight because we had a secret weapon. He was a flat-out crazy kid, our weapon, and small, about ninety pounds—ten whole pounds more than me; I was a little guy, myself. But man, that kid had some muscles. With his clothes on, he was Clark Kent, but when the shirt came off, you were looking at Superman. He was strong and fearless, and he could hold his own, but those Fifth Avenue kids were nasty and dirty, and they had a few cats who could really fight.

Our Superman took off his shirt and flew into the middle of the fray, and one of their little guys followed suit. These two shirtless cats went at it for a few minutes, at which point the Fifth Avenue kid, blood trickling from his lip, held up his hands and said, "Okay, man. You win." Superman dropped his defense, and one second later their guy went to town. Turned out that, unbeknownst to us, their guy had been taking boxing lessons from a professional fighter. Superman ended up on the ground in a full nelson, and he cried out, "Ain't none of you gonna help me, man?"

We were all in such shock from the brutality of the attack that we hadn't moved in to defend our brother; his plea for help snapped us out of our stupor. One of the crazy guys from our side ran over to a garbage can and went through the mess until he found a milk bottle. After he broke the bottle and went after the boxer, well, suffice it to say that I haven't seen fighting like that either before or since.

A quick aside: I don't recall the specific film, but I remember hearing in some movie theater or another that before a police officer opens fire on somebody, he or she has to give three warnings: "Halt, or I'll shoot, first warning! Halt, or I'll shoot, second warning! Halt, or I'll shoot, final warning!" And then, *pop, pop, pop, pop, pop!* Either that was a flat-out lie, or it didn't apply on Fifth Avenue in Pittsburgh.

When the cops rolled up, they were locked and loaded, and didn't give us a single warning. We heard the doors slam, the shoes on the pavement, and the gunfire: *pop, pop, pop, pop, pop!* At first, I counted the shots—no idea why—but soon lost track. I ran away, but I heard one of my friends screaming and ran right back—he'd been hit in the ankle and was lying on the ground, writhing in pain. I knelt down to help him, and next thing I know, I'm on the ground myself.

Before I could do anything, a cop came out of nowhere, grabbed me, and swooped me off the pavement. His partner ran over and patted me up and down. "Where'd I hit you?" he said, running his hands up and down my chest. I don't know if he was scared that he'd shot me or relieved.

I said, "You didn't hit me, man. I don't feel nothing."

He looked at my face, then said, "There it is."

I touched my forehead, and there was a little gash. "Man, that's nothing," I said.

"It's not nothing, kid. You got hit with a bullet from a thirty-eight." (Today, if you look really hard at my head, you can see the tiny scar. Later on, I asked a doctor how come I wasn't killed, and he said, "Thirty-eights are built to stop you, not kill you.")

And that's how I ended up with a six-week tour at Thorn Hill, one of Pittsburgh's most notorious reform schools.

Reform school, man, that was an eye-opener. Everything about it was bleak, *everything*, the ghetto version of a Charles Dickens novel. Each day you had to fight, whether you wanted to or not . . . and the negative energy in there was such that you did, indeed, want to fight. Violence and anger felt like a natural part of the environment, and you got used to it, so much so that after a while, you didn't feel it anymore, and you stopped caring about anything. For that matter, it got to the point where I was the first guy to get a lick in, and that worked in my favor, because nobody expected that sort of aggression from a little guy like me. So let's say one of the inmates—it wasn't jail, but it sure felt like it, so I thought of us as inmates—started in with me about, say, changing the channel on the television, I'd pretend to go crazy: "Man, if you touch that dial, I'm gonna mess you up! We're watching channel five, and if you've got a problem with it . . . ," and so on. Inevitably, somebody somewhere *would* have a problem with it, and we'd start to rumble like crazy.

When you're incarcerated, wherever you are—reform school, prison, whatever—there are rules, none of which are written; you have to figure it out as you go along. And I broke a few of them on my first day inside.

It was lunch, and I was sitting at a table with fifteen other cats, pushing my food around the plate. Out of the corner of my eye, I saw a man, a *huge* Caucasian man, we're talking about 240 pounds huge. I couldn't stomach much of that lunch, so I scraped my almost-full plate into the garbage. I sat back down at the table, but before I could even get settled, the huge guy flew across the room—I couldn't believe how fast he moved—lifted me out of the chair, and slapped me silly. As blood spurted from my lip, I felt dizzy, almost to the point of blacking out. "If you wanted something different to eat," he yelled, "why didn't you just ask for it?" Then he dragged me back up to my room, threw me in, and locked the door. Hours later, somebody brought me an ice cream bar. That was my dinner.

Day after day, all we did was fight. If you didn't fight, if you didn't come across as tough, and if you weren't tough—if you didn't defend yourself, and defend yourself *well*—man, you were in some serious trouble. All we did every day was fight, even on your birthday. The day I turned fifteen, one of the men in charge, Mr. Hartman, asked me, "Why do you fight so much, Benson?"

I didn't answer.

"Today's your birthday, isn't it?" he asked. "Are we gonna have any trouble out of you today?"

"No, Mr. Hartman."

"You like fighting so much, you want to fight me?"

Again, I didn't answer.

He said, "Right. Come on. Let's do this." Hartman took me in a room somewhere in the bowels of the school, took off his sports coat, loosened his tie, and said, "You think you're so tough? You wanna show me how bad you are? Let's go."

From behind me, somebody said, "Now, John, don't hurt that little boy."

I looked over my shoulder, and there's a woman sitting in a rocking chair, knitting a sweater. It was Hartman's wife.

Hartman listened to his wife. He didn't hurt me. Much.

At the end of those six weeks, I was more or less reformed, and I say "more or less" because my first day back on the street, I got into another fight. But after that fight was finished, I decided enough was enough. I was going to stay away from violence, stay out of trouble, and stay out of jail.

The next day, my cousin and I started a doo-wop group called the Altairs, and my whole life changed.

3 Those Doo-Wop Sounds

Nobody can say with exact certainty when doo-wop became doo-wop. Some believe the first doo-wop group was the Ink Spots, a quartet out of Indianapolis. They started making music in the mid-1930s and went over the moon in 1939 with "If I Didn't Care," a ballad that still sounds relevant and beautiful today. Other folks point to the Mills Brothers out of Ohio, who hit the scene a couple years before the Ink Spots. It's possible that the Mills Brothers had a direct influence on the Ink Spots, but it's also possible that the two groups hit on a similar style around the same time, which wouldn't be out of the realm of possibility. For example, think about Charlie Parker and Dizzy Gillespie: Bird was playing bebop-sounding chord changes and rhythms in the Jay McShann Orchestra in Kansas City in 1938, while Diz was heading in a similar musical direction out on the East Coast. In the late 1940s and early 1950s, doo-wop went mainstream, and a whole bunch of vocal quartets made a whole bunch of noise all over the country. There were the Swallows, the Ravens, the Cadillacs, the Fleetwoods, the Larks, the Impalas, Little Anthony and the Imperials, the Crows, and the Edsels, to name a few. (Seems like they were all named after birds or cars, doesn't it?)

When I was fifteen, my awareness of doo-wop was, well, I wasn't all that aware. I knew a fair amount about jazz and a whole lot about the music you heard on the radio and in the movies, but I didn't know a thing about vocal groups. Today, I'm kind of an authority, and if life were different—if the guitar hadn't become such an important part of my being—who knows, I might've spent the last five or so decades leading a vocal quartet, because being part of the Altairs was a ball.

The Altairs was a quintet, consisting of Nathaniel Benson—we called him Nanny—who was my cousin on my mother's side; Ralph Terry, who handled all the low parts; William Herndon, who had as pretty of a tenor voice as you'll find; and Richard Harris, the youngest member of the band, whose father, Raymond, was one of the more interesting cats in Pittsburgh. (Please permit me a quick digression about Raymond Harris. This cat played so many instruments that I can't even remember which ones; let's just say he played them all. He taught Ray Brown and Paul Chambers how to swing on upright bass. He taught Stanley Turrentine how to blow that strong, strong tenor saxophone. He even taught Art Blakey a thing or two about drums . . . although it would've been hard to give Buhaina any drum tips, because he knew it all. Raymond took these and many other kids off the streets; it was a jazz boys' club. Raymond was a forceful man, who'd tell these heavies, "Mannnnn, you guys ain't gonna be no musicians. You ain't gonna be *nothing*. You can't even read no music! Now me, I can play. I can play better than any of you." Imagine saying that to Ray, or Paul, or Stan, or Bu. Just imagine. That's like my high school art teacher telling Picasso, "Mannnnn, you ain't never gonna sell a painting to nobody. Who's gonna pay good money for something by a cat who can't even get a face right?" But that was Raymond Harris for you. Later on down the line, Richard's mother became our manager, because sometimes it's a good idea to keep it in the family.) Now no two people in the world are exactly alike, but the Altairs, man, we were as different as you could get—nobody's ever seen a crew like us. But we came together when we needed to because we had two things in common: our love for music and our ghetto childhood. We knew what rough was. We knew what ugly was. We knew what poverty was. We knew what struggling was. We knew what *nothing* was. But we also knew what good music was.

The Altairs didn't get off to an auspicious start; shortly into our first appearance, we were laughed offstage. But we were tough and weren't about to let one impolite audience derail us, so we put our heads down, kept rehearsing, kept gigging, and kept improving, and soon enough, we were one of the top vocal groups in the area . . . if not *the* top group. (I can't give you any exact numbers, but from what I could tell at our shows, we had more fans than *anybody*.) We even managed to cut a record, "Groovy Time," a bouncy, mid-tempo thing that had a lot of whoa-whoa-whoas and lyrics like, "When I take my girl to her door, I'm gonna squeeze her with all of my might. / I'm gonna kiss her lips while my heart does flips." We moved a few copies, and even though "groovy time" was a slick saying, we didn't sell enough to the point that we were able to make another one. But it was a good notch in my belt, and it gave me some more invaluable experience in the recording studio.

We became one of the busiest doo-wop groups in the tri-state area of Pennsylvania, Ohio, and West Virginia, and since we performed so often—and since much of our repertoire consisted of the popular music of the day, or the week, or the month—I learned how to emulate all the great singers. (Eventually, we sounded good enough that we were hired to open for the Miracles, as in Smokey Robinson and the Miracles.) At the beginning of our set, I'd have to sound like Frankie Lymon, and at the end, it would be Tony Williams from the Platters. That's the sort of lesson you'll never get at school, or from a private teacher, or even from listening to "The Great Pretender" or "My Prayer" over and over again. When you're onstage and singing (or playing your instrument) for paying customers, it's your job to give your best, to give them what they expect—or even what they *don't* expect—and in this case, the paying customers weren't looking to hear Little Georgie Benson be Little Georgie Benson. They wanted to hear the Altairs sing the songs from the groups they'd otherwise never be able to hear in concert. See, many of the big groups didn't make it to Pennsylvania, Ohio, and West Virginia, so we had to make certain we were the next best thing. This all taught me the importance of consistency, hard work, and respecting your audiences. Throughout my playing career, I've made it a point to deliver the best show I can, regardless of the venue, the repertoire, the sound system, or the size of the crowd. I don't care if the gig is at a straw hut in the middle of a jungle, the only amplification is a megaphone made from a piece of cardboard, and the crowd numbers four. If these folks paid their hard-earned money to hear me play "On Broadway," I'm going to play "On Broadway," and I'm going to play the heck out of it.

While we Altairs were off doing our vocal thing, the electric guitar was on its way to becoming one of the most vital pieces of American popular music, possibly *the* most vital piece. Bill Doggett's "Honky Tonk," for instance, wasn't just a popular song—it was *important*. Doggett was an organist, but in my mind, the best part of the song was the guitar solo, which I found out much later came courtesy of the song's co-composer, the great Philadelphia master Billy Butler. In-the-know jazz folks will remember Billy for the albums he cut for Prestige in the late 1960s and early 1970s—*Guitar Soul* and *Night Life* are both good places to start—but it was his solo on "Honky Tonk" that put him on the map. And even if you didn't know his name—and most people didn't know his name, because record companies tended not to list sidemen on the sleeve of their 45s—believe me, you knew the solo. By the time Billy made his statement—a statement filled with blue notes, bent strings, and glorious held tones—the grease would be dripping from your speakers.

The thing is, the Altairs had to hire a guitar player, because in those days, I couldn't sing and play at the same time . . . and I *especially* couldn't simultaneously sing *and* play *and* dance. And dancing was essential, because any self-respecting doo-wop or R&B group had plenty of steps. So we hired this guitar player, and he was a nice cat and all, but problem was, he couldn't really play. I had to show him *everything*.

Here's a typical rehearsal: We'd introduce a new tune, and he'd play the wrong changes. I'd grab his guitar and say, "Let me show you here. It goes like this." *Bling.* He'd say, "Got it." We'd start over, then, *Blong,* wrong chord. I'd take the guitar back and say, "No, man, it's like this." *Blingggg.* We'd start yet again, then, *Grrrrrink,* wrong chord. "Give me that back, man," I'd say, yanking away his axe. "The chord looks like *this.*" And so on and so on and so on.

Time and again, the guys in the group would say, "George, why don't you just play the guitar?"

Time and again, I'd tell them, "I can't do all that and sing."

"Yes, you can. And even if you can't do it perfectly, it's better than going through this."

They finally convinced me to start taking the instrument seriously, but there was one huge problem: I didn't have a guitar. I cried about it to my mother—"Ma, I got to have a guitar. I need a guitar"—to no avail.

One afternoon, I saw a guitar in the window of the pawnshop right next door to Spokane's, and man, I loved the looks of it, even though it was obvious to me even at that age that it wasn't particularly well constructed. It was cute, it was little, and it was yellow. And I wanted it, but it cost fifty-five dollars. Sure, I was making money with my various endeavors, but fifty-five dollars was a fortune.

When I told my stepfather about the instrument, Tom nodded and said, "Take me down there and show it to me." So I took him down, but he didn't even go inside the store. He just peered into the window, gave it a look-see from all angles, and said, "I can make that."

I said, "*What?*"

"Yeah, you just have to draw me a picture of the guitar, then I'll put it together."

I'd been taking some commercial art classes at Connelly Vocational, so drawing it wasn't a problem. When I finished, Tom traced the shape onto my mother's oak hope chest, where she kept all her blankets and knickknacks. He then cut out the shape with a coping saw—and for you folks who don't use tools all that much, that's one of those saws with a thin handle, a thinner blade, and an upside-down U-shaped frame. It took an entire day, and he went through twenty blades, but he got the shape *down*. He then surfaced it with this stuff I'd never heard of called Formica—you don't see too many guitars made out of Formica, do you?—then scored twenty-three dollars' worth of electronics and strings, and there it was, Little Georgie Benson's first guitar. I plugged it into an amplifier, not knowing if it would work, and knowing even less if it would sound good. But sure enough, when I strummed it, *Brrrrrrrrrring*, darned if it didn't sound like a real live instrument.

Our first gig after I became the proud owner of a guitar was at a nearby record hop. Neither my stepfather nor I knew how to make a case, so I carried the axe in a shopping bag, the neck sticking out long and straight, like the tail of an angry cat. When I wandered in, the disc jockey, Porky Chadnick, was playing "Let's Go to the Dance" by the Robins—you know that one: "Let's go, let's go, let's go, let's go to the daaaaaannnnce"—and when he saw me, he took it off on the quick, scratching the record along the way.

When the music stopped, a bunch of the kids, annoyed that their dancing was interrupted for no apparent reason, started yelling, "What's going on here? *What's going on?*"

Chadnick called to me, "What do you have in the shopping bag, kid?"

"A guitar," I said kind of sheepishly, then took it out of the bag.

He gave me an approving nod, then said, "Where did you get that guitar from?"

"My father made it for me."

His jaw dropped. "Made it? You didn't buy it at a music store? This is amazing!" He then asked the crowd, "What do you all think of that?" Everybody clapped, and I was proud as could be. They clapped even harder and louder when I took the stage with the band, plugged in, and *Brrrrrrrrrring*. It was a crude instrument, but it made enough music to get folks dancing and clapping. And I even knew then that if you can get people to dance and clap, you're doing something right.

About a year later, I was ready for another axe, so I decided to make my own. Being that I was at a vocational high school, I figured I could make a better instrument if I used as many of my resources as possible—and in that case, those resources were my fellow students. I had friends in different classes who had different skill sets: I gave one of them a piece of wood and a drawing, and told him, "Cut this out for me with your band saw, and don't forget to cut the hole." When he was done, I brought it to another pal and told him, "Sand this down for me good. Come on, man, sand it *good*." (I was eager to get it done, so I might've been a bit more aggressive than necessary.) When he was done, I told another, "Put some black lacquer on it." Then I brought in the fingerboard and told another, "Why don't you put some holes on the top of this for some tuning pegs? Then stick the fingerboard on the body." Every day, I'd come in with a different part—a tailpiece, a bridge, some wiring—and some new directions. My friends thought I was nuts.

Finally, it was ready, and it looked beautiful: black, smooth, shiny, professional, ready for action. I brought it to school, along with my amplifier. The whole class gathered around as I prepared to make some noise. The room was silent. Everybody stared at me, the guitar, and the amp. The kids were tense, nervous, and excited all at once . . . just like me. I tuned up, plugged in, and strummed: *Bllllllllllllllin-nnnnnnng.* It worked! And it sounded great! The whole class went crazy, applauding and whistling. "Yeah, man! . . . That's *baaaaad* stuff! . . . Congratulations, Georgie! . . . I never thought you'd get it to work, but man, you got it to work!"

That was the last guitar I ever made.

Word got out around Pittsburgh that I was playing some pretty good music on an instrument I'd made (more or less) by myself, and it seemed like everybody wanted to hear me play. But I gave them my standard rap: "Man, I'm a singer. I play a little guitar, but I'm not a guitar player. I'm a singer."

They'd inevitably say, "You play good enough." Maybe I did and maybe I didn't, but I figured it wouldn't hurt to give it a shot, to try to become as good of an instrumentalist as I was a vocalist. The thing is, I had to learn songs . . . a *lot* of songs, songs like the aforementioned "Honky Tonk." I studied that record as hard as anything I'd ever studied, and picked up every single one of Billy Butler's licks, and not just the licks, but everything inside, outside, and next to the licks: the blue notes, the bends, the whole tones, *everything*. And if you were a guitar player, you couldn't go onstage without knowing surf rock tunes like "Walk, Don't Run" by the Ventures—which, by the way, was originally recorded by Johnny Smith, a tried and true jazz cat—and "Rumble" by Link Wray, so those soon became part of my growing repertoire. (Johnny Smith, by the way, is the definition of an unsung hero, a cat who developed his own sound while all the other cats were scuffling, trying to get their stuff together. He'd hit one note, and it would ring forever. I always wondered why he could do that and I couldn't.)

As was the case when I was with the doo-wop group, being forced to play different tunes by different composers and different styles played a crucial role in helping me become a well-rounded musician—for that matter, it helped me become a well-rounded person, and that's something I feel is a vital component of quality art: the ability to play and feel comfortable in a variety of styles and settings. So while I was still singing with the Altairs, I started learning all these little crazy tunes, tunes that I might not have otherwise learned. But though our school was desegregated, it wasn't *that* desegregated; there were considerably more white folks than black, so it would stand to reason that the Ventures and Link Wray would be more in demand than Bill Doggett. As I wasn't prejudiced about any styles, I was happy to learn them all, and since my ear had gotten pretty good, I could figure out all their crazy tunes, which most everybody considered to be a minor miracle. The more I learned, the more I wanted to learn, and I knew that listening to records would only get me so far. When I heard a new hot guitarist was coming to town, I'd track him down, go to his hotel, and wake him out of a sound sleep with a barrage of questions about his approach to the instrument. Some of them were flattered, and some of them were annoyed. But without fail, they answered my questions.

I got good, and the fact that I was becoming an honest-to-goodness instrumentalist helped me win a lot of friends, because, as it turns out, people dig hanging out with the guitar player. And I needed all the friends I could get, because even though I was reformed, I still had my fair share of enemies and, thus, my fair share of fights.

I won some of those fights, and I lost some, but whenever I fought with one of the white boys, no matter who won, they'd want to shake hands. Whenever it happened—and it happened a lot—I'd say, "Shake hands? Man, I won't shake hands with *nobody*."

"Shake hands," they'd insist.

"No way, man. I'm not shaking hands. No way, no how."

This would go on until I finally gave in and gave their offered mitt a quick up-and-down pump. It was a different way of thinking, a way of thinking that deep down I knew I'd need to get used to. Years later, I ran into one of those cats, and he asked me, "George, remember that fight we had?"

"I don't." I fought a lot, and most of them ran together in my memory.

"Well, George, we did rumble, and I know we had problems, but you're my friend, and you always will be." That was unexpected, to say the least. I wouldn't have expected a cat I smacked around to give me a metaphorical peace pipe. But I'm probably not the only guy who had this sort of experience. I know Jimi Hendrix used to fight. I know Prince used to fight. And I know they were enlightened cats, and if I were a betting man, I'd wager that they had similarly revelatory experiences. It must be a guitar player thing.

Those fights could've been a lot worse for my opponents, because even though I was short, I was strong, and I could outrun and out-hit most anybody. But I wasn't the strongest small black kid in the neighborhood—that would be Sylvester Harris. Sylvester—whom everybody on the street called Poopadoo—was built like Superman and could do two hundred push-ups like it was nothing. Poopadoo was an angry cat, and never ran from a fight. It got to the point where nobody wanted to fight us anyhow. We were little guys, but we were toughies, so most everybody respected us. Eventually, we grew up and cut out that sort of nonsense.

The building in which my family lived was right across the street from Connelly, which was helpful when the Altairs had a late gig on a school night; any kind of significant addition to my commute could've brought the whole thing tumbling down. It all came to a head when the city finally decided to break ground on an arena they'd been threatening to build for twenty-odd years.

The first thing they did was buy all the houses in the neighborhood for peanuts—I think the entire hotel went for $150—then condemn the property and kick us out. I watched them tear down our building and destroy our street. Nobody would call our neighborhood paradise, but it was *our* neighborhood, and when somebody takes something that's yours, regardless of how much you like or dislike it, it hurts.

On the plus side, we moved into the new projects that were a quarter-mile away . . . and this was before *projects* became a synonym for *ghetto*. Our projects were what projects were supposed to be: affordable, safe, respectable housing for underprivileged families. The building was new, the hallways were pristine, and the apartments were spotless. For us, it was like we moved to heaven.

The problem was that we were considerably farther away from Connelly, which meant I had to walk from my house in the projects across town every morning; and on those early Monday mornings after those late weekend nights, I was exhausted to the point that I fell asleep in the majority of my classes. That didn't stop me from getting all As and B pluses on my report cards, but it didn't do wonders for my reputation among my teachers.

One morning during my senior year, while I was snoring away during art class, my art teacher clapped his hands right by my ear.

When I woke up with a start, he asked, "George, why are you always sleeping in class?"

Before I answered, I looked him right in the eye and thought, *Man, this cat is a trip.* He wasn't the most attractive guy, what with his gigantic schnoz and the bumps all over his face. He was a heavy smoker, and whenever he stepped out of the class to take a puff, he'd come back trailing smoke juice so heavily that the entire classroom stunk. His method of teaching wasn't really a method . . . nor was it really teaching: He'd have one of the students stand in front of the class, then we'd do a drawing. That was supposed to teach us how to be an artist.

One day he stood up in front of the class and said, "The subject today is . . . *me.*" That was our test, to draw him.

So I drew him, big schnoz, face bumps, and all. He wandered up and down the aisles, grading along the way: "Nice job, that's a B plus . . . Hmm, I don't know about that, that's a C . . . That's terrible, D minus." When he got to my desk, he looked at my drawing, then at me, then at the drawing, then back at me. "So you think that's what I look like?" he asked.

"I just drew what I saw," I said. "You've got a big schnoz. I can't do nothin' about that."

He looked at me, then the drawing, then at me some more, then busted out laughing. "A-plus," he said, then held up the picture and said, "Look, kids!" Everybody laughed like crazy.

Finally, after an inordinate amount of time—remember, I'd just woken up—I answered his question, "I worked last night," I said. "I'm in a singing group. I have to make money to help support my folks."

He shook his head and said, "Listen, you have to make up your mind whether you want to go to school or play music."

I said, "Oh, man, that ain't no contest. I'm out of here." And that's why I didn't graduate high school. My mother wasn't thrilled, to say the least. She really wanted me to have that diploma, because it would be the first step in the direction of the profession she'd chosen for me: doctor.

Eighteen years later, in 1978, while I was in Pittsburgh for a gig, I ran into a friend from Connelly. After some reminiscing, he said, "Remember graduation, George? That was special," he said.

I said. "Well, you graduated. I didn't."

"Are you sure?" he asked. "I saw your picture in the yearbook."

He was right about that. Before I left school, I'd had my graduation photos taken. "I'm sure," I told him.

"Hmm. I have an idea."

"What's that?"

"Tomorrow afternoon, let's go back up to Connelly and have some lunch in the lunchroom, just for old time's sake."

"Sounds good to me."

The next day, we went to Connelly, just as planned. When we got out of the elevator on the lunchroom floor, there were hundreds of people crammed into the room, some of whom were from the press, and all of whom were cheering. All of my old teachers were there . . . except for that art teacher. The vice principal stepped forward, clutching a piece of paper. "George, we have something for you. I believe you forgot to pick this up when you left." And then he handed me a diploma.

That was one of the greatest days of my life.

Now I'm not condoning my choice to not graduate. It just happened to work for me, but that was due to the musical climate, my life circumstances, and some fortuitous timing—in terms of my musical growth, I couldn't have left school at a better time. See, the guitar had embedded itself in my brain and my heart to the point that it drew me away from the Altairs. I was afraid that if I hung in there, it would be ten more years of scuffling for work, playing small-to-medium-sized venues, and living hand to mouth, and that didn't appeal to me.

So once I was done with school, I formed my own band, called the All Stars. (Talk about delusions of grandeur!) The first cat I recruited to join the group was a friend who, for reasons that will soon be apparent, shall remain nameless. This nameless friend was a guitar player, but since I only needed one guitarist in the group, my stepfather took his axe, grabbed some tools, and turned it into a bass guitar. The problem was, soon after we began gigging, the guy went out and robbed a bank, so we became known as Little George Benson and His Bank Robbers. We didn't last long.

Note that this was 1960, an important year in jazz history because it was right around the rise of the organ trio.

Up until then, the vast majority of jazz trios at your local club consisted of piano, bass, and drums. That was a sound that everybody was used to, that everybody was comfortable with, be it Thelonious Monk with Percy Heath on bass and Art Blakey on drums, or Bud Powell with Curly Russell and Max Roach, or Oscar Peterson with Ray Brown and Ed Thigpen. But the organ was always hiding in the weeds, waiting to pounce. Fats Waller played a bit of organ in the mid-1920s, and while his work on the instrument was swinging in its own way, it wasn't accessible enough to convince other pianists to try their hand at it. Count Basie gave it a shot in the late 1930s, and while his work on the instrument was swinging as all get-out, it still didn't popularize the darn thing. Milt Buckner, a keyboardist out of St. Louis, opened some ears in the early 1950s when he switched to organ after a few years of playing piano with Lionel Hampton's band. And then there was Wild Bill Davis, one of the first organists I remember hearing, and he was probably the first cat who played modern jazz organ, although his records were as much blues as they were jazz. But when Jimmy Smith came onto the scene in the mid-1950s, man, all bets were off.

The thing about Jimmy was that he could combine swing, blues, and bebop, all within twelve bars, and make it sound seamless. Not only that, but he used the Hammond B-3 to its fullest, squeezing every possible sound out of the instrument, switching from one setting to the next in order to suit either the song or the moment. If he played a ballad, he'd use a full sound with lots of vibrato; and if he played the blues, he'd go for greasy; and if he played bop, it was a staccato, flat feel, in order to make certain that the listener could hear every note of every run. And man, that brother played *fast*, faster than any organist to that point. He was a true innovator, the Louis Armstrong of the organ, a cat who could be both an entertainer— and if you were lucky enough to catch him live in his heyday, you know that he was as entertaining as any jazz musician you'll ever see—and a serious musician. Considering his influence on the era and the instrument, he probably doesn't get his just due.

Between 1956 and 1958, Jimmy recorded over a dozen albums, most of which featured him playing alongside a guitarist and a drummer . . . and no bassist. The guitarist was usually Thornel Schwartz, who hailed from Philadelphia and was another cat who didn't get the recognition he deserved. Even at my tender age, I recognized that Thornel had that *something*, so later on down the line, I took some lessons with him—good teacher, funny cat. Eddie McFadden was another one of Smitty's go-to guitar guys, and Kenny Burrell, that great player from Detroit, was yet another. Jimmy's first regular drummer was Donald Bailey, but Don Gardner was the guy who, to me, was the most important. More about Don later.

So why no bassist? Well, Jimmy and Wild Bill and Bill Doggett and Baby Face Willette and Larry Young and Brother Jack McDuff and Shirley Scott and all the other up-and-coming organists played the bass notes with their foot, using the pedals to replicate as best they could what they imagined an upright bassist would do on any given tune. The reason for this was twofold: First, it gave the organ trio its funky, trademark sound. The organ's bass notes were rounder and more sustained than those of an upright bass, which led to a greasier feel. Second, it saved the bandleader money. If the organ grinder could cover the bass, he wouldn't have to pay another cat. All of which was why in 1960, club owners were jonesing to hire organ trios: The sound was popular and the bands were affordable. It all added up to extra bread in everybody's pocket, so suddenly, just like that, guitar players who knew a little bit of jazz and a lot of blues were in demand.

After the Bank Robbers ran its course, I worked in an organ group led by a cat named Bob Storey. At first, we were a standard organ/guitar/drums unit, but when he added a saxophonist, man, my world opened up. The saxophonist played all these smooth runs that sounded like nothing I'd ever heard: It was swinging and soulful, but it was also modern and melodic. One night soon after he joined the group, I asked him, "What kind of music is that you're playing? I like it!"

He said, "Come over to my house. I'll show you what's what."

The saxophonist was an older man, and he had lots of children who ran roughshod over his home. Once he got the kids to bed, he put on a Billie Holiday record—it might've been "Fine and Mellow" or possibly "The Man I Love"—and said, "Listen to what's going on behind her."

And sure enough, there it was, that tenor sax sound that I fell in love with. I said, "That's it!"

"Yeah," he said. "I'm into Prez."

"Prez?" I asked. "Who's that?"

"You don't know Prez? You don't know Lester Young?" He explained to me that Lester—whose nickname was Prez because his fans believed him to be the president of the saxophone—made his name as a member of the Count Basie Orchestra. He was another cat who could play any and all styles and tempos—swing, blues, bebop, ballads, *everything*—with equal aplomb, which meant that listeners and musicians of all ages and eras could relate and appreciate what he was about . . . even a seventeen-year-old from Pittsburgh who was raised on doo-wop.

After I left Bob's band, I started another group of my own, and since I'd gotten used to the saxophone/organ sound, I hired a sax player, a cat my own age named Larry Smith, from Aliquippa, Pennsylvania, just about five miles out of Pittsburgh. Larry was a great guy and a great musician, but he had a tendency to play all kinds of weird stuff. I recognized that his technique was impeccable and his musical colors were good, but man, he played a lot of notes, and a lot of those notes flat-out didn't make sense, especially in the context of our repertoire. See, we were strictly an R&B band, and the stuff Larry played, well, most of it wasn't R&B.

One night, after a particularly late gig at a club that was closer to Aliquippa than it was to Pittsburgh, Larry noticed I was exhausted, so he said, "George, it's late. Before you get behind that wheel, you're going to have a cup of coffee, then you're coming to my house." Which is exactly what I did. The second we got inside, I collapsed onto the couch, and Larry put on a record—a quiet record, a record unlike any I'd ever heard.

"Man," I said, "that's beautiful." You could call it a fast ballad or a slow swinger, and it featured an alto saxophonist floating above a lush orchestra. The arrangement was as straight-ahead as could be, but the sax player was filling up the space and playing lots of notes. And, as was the case with Larry, some of those notes were weird, but in the orchestral context, they made more sense.

Halfway through the tune, I asked, "What is that, man? What am I listening to?"

Larry said, "That's Charlie Parker. The song is called 'Just Friends,' and the album is called *Bird with Strings*. Bird was Parker's nickname. He passed away a few years back."

I said, "Who the heck is Charlie Parker?" The name sounded familiar, but I couldn't quite place it.

"*You don't know who Charlie Parker is?*" he asked, incredulous. "Man, sit your butt down and listen to this again!" And I did. And I *really* listened. And my entire life changed. By the time Parker made it through the melody, I understood that was the way music should be. The gorgeous arrangement, the complex harmonies, the heartfelt vibe, and the tangible emotion all combined to create something that even my untrained ears knew wasn't just a song but a piece of art.

(Later on, I learned how to hum Parker's solo, and having that under my belt made everything else I played or sang easier. Sometimes folks will say to me, "Man, that thing you did in the middle of 'On Broadway' sounded impossible." I'll tell them, "Trust me, that ain't nothing compared to Charlie Parker's 'Just Friends.'" And I'm not the only person who feels that *Bird with Strings* is one of the albums that sums up what jazz is all about, what with its complex yet accessible arrangements, its combination of gorgeous strings and driving big band, and Parker's intense, thoughtful solos. "April in Paris," "Summertime," "I Didn't Know What Time It Was"—each song told a story. And thank goodness I was hipped to Bird, because you can't be great unless you know what greatness is.)

I said to Larry, "Man, I want to play like that."

"Man," Larry said, "*everybody* wants to play like that!"

After the third time through the album, I remembered a conversation I had with Tom Collier one afternoon while I was practicing. He listened to me for a few minutes, then said, "What's with all that 'We want Cantor' stuff you're playing?"

I had zero idea what he was talking about. "What do you mean by 'We want Cantor'?" I asked.

"You ever heard of Eddie Cantor?" he asked. Before I could answer, he said, "He's a Broadway superstar. Sometimes he would take too long to get on the bandstand, and the crowd would start chanting, 'We want Cantor! We want Cantor!' It got to be such a common thing that the band started to accompany the crowd, and they'd play a melody and some chord changes to go along with it." He hummed the melody, and it was a simple structure, the basis of almost every R&B song we played. He said, "That's what I mean by 'We want Cantor.' You don't have to play it that way."

I said, "Well, that's the way the song goes. I mean, how should I play it? That's the way it's written."

He said, "You can play something different from that. You can play anything you want."

I asked, "Like what?"

"Listen to Charlie Parker," he said.

I said, "That ain't telling me nothing."

He said, "Play chromatics."

"Chromatics?" I asked. "What the heck are chromatics?"

He hummed me a chromatic scale. If you want to know what it sounds like, go to a piano, hit a key, then hit the key right next to that, then the next one, then the next one, and so on.

That wasn't a funky or bluesy sound, certainly not the kind of thing you'd hear at your typical R&B gig. I shook my head. "No. No sir. No way. That ain't working. That won't work."

"It depends on how you use them, George," he said. "Use them in the right place at the right time, and it'll work like a charm."

"Not where I play, man. Not at the bars."

He shook his head and said, "Just listen to Charlie Parker. It'll make sense then." (Note: When I heard *Bird with Strings* all those months later, it made a little more sense. It took a little bit of time for it to totally click.) Me and my stepfather, we used to argue about chromatics all the time: He wanted me to use them, and I wanted to stick with what I knew worked.

That is, until I started going to jam sessions.

We had a guy in our neighborhood named Chad Evans. (For some reason, he went by Carrie rather than Chad.) Like the sax player from Bob Storey's group, Carrie had a house full of children, babies everywhere, but on Saturdays he would allow all of us musicians in the neighborhood to come to his house and listen to, discuss, and play music. Carrie went out of his way to make us feel grown up; he spoke to us like adults, he treated us like adults, and he gave us adult drinks. They weren't *good* adult drinks, mind you—we're talking cheap beer and even cheaper wine—but we weren't supposed to be drinking *anything*, so it was cool.

He played us all the latest jazz records, a lot of which featured guitar players who were playing at a high level beyond a higher level.

At Carrie's place, I heard Kenny Burrell for the first time, and man, did that make an impression. Here was a guy only a few years older than me, and the way he attacked his axe, well, it sounded like he'd been doing it for decades. There was one record in particular, just called *Kenny Burrell*, and it was on the Prestige label. The cats in the rhythm section were all from Detroit, too—Tommy Flanagan on piano, Doug Watkins on bass, and Elvin Jones on drums—and, like Kenny, they sounded like veterans, but they had a young energy that I could relate to, even though I didn't quite understand everything they were playing. What I did know, what I fully understood, was that Kenny had some serious chops, and he had licks to spare. They did a rendition of "All of You," and it reminded me of *Bird with Strings* in that it sizzled even though the tempo was slow and mellow. And that Elvin Jones, man, even then—even with those untrained ears of mine—I could tell he was a monster.

Carrie also introduced me to Grant Green, a guy not much older than me, and there was another cat who was doing things I'd never heard. He was on a record by an organist named Sam Lazar called *Space Flight*. Since most of the tunes on the album were traditional 12-bar blues—a format with which I was quite familiar—I related to the music, but what Grant was doing on those 12-bar blues was radical. See, he made his guitar *sing*. Even when he was playing a fast run, each note was played with care and love. You could tell that he left nothing to chance. He knew where his fingers were going four measures before they got there.

And then there was Hank Garland, a country kid from South Carolina. And when I say "country," I'm not just talking about his hometown—the cat played unbelievable country music, as well as country-tinged rock 'n' roll. Carrie explained that Hank had recorded with everybody from Elvis Presley to Roy Orbison to the Everly Brothers, but he also played jazz. He said, "I saw this album of his, *Jazz Winds from a New Direction*, and the cover had him in the back seat of a convertible, and there were all these guitars sticking out of the car. When I saw it, I thought, 'Well, maybe he's good.'" And then he put the record on, and there was that *fire*, that *sound*, and it hit me in the same manner as Charlie Christian. (I met Hank several years later, and he became one of my mentors. He was as great of a man as he was a guitarist—and that's saying something.)

And then there was this other new cat, Wes Montgomery. More about him in a bit.

Sometimes after he played us a certain record, Carrie tried to teach us how to play what we were hearing, but he wasn't the kind of teacher who'd put some sheet music in front of you and show you the guts of the song. His method was more along the lines of, "Look at my fingers, man. Now put your finger over here." But we picked it up, and thank goodness, because he was teaching us stuff we would probably never learn anywhere else.

Eventually, I picked up enough from Carrie that I felt comfortable going to jam sessions, much to the chagrin of most every musician in Pittsburgh. See, I was still known as a singer, and back then, the women, they swooned over the boy vocalists. So I'd go up onstage with my guitar, ready to take a swing at whatever the other cats on the bandstand wanted to throw me, and when the girls saw me, they called out, "Georgie! Little Georgie Benson! Sing us something! Stop playing that guitar and start singing!" and ignored all the other cats.

Everybody else onstage—the piano player, the bass player, the drummer, *everybody*—felt slighted, and they'd grumble under their breath, "I hate that kid. I hate it when he comes in here. I hate that Little Georgie Benson." But it wasn't *that* far under their breath; I heard every word they said. They never made me feel welcome, and I didn't get a whole lot out of being there.

But there was one guy who let me come to his house for his Saturday jam sessions, a sax player whose name has long since been forgotten. At first, he literally just let me come to his house—not *in* the house, *to* the house. Word started getting around that I was growing as a guitar player, so one day, he put his hand on my shoulder and said, "Come on in and play something." That was a big deal, man, to be accepted and welcomed by cats who knew how to *play*, to *really* play. I could play the blues—heck, with a little practice, *anybody* could play the blues—but not many could play the blues *well*, and I was determined to become the best blues player that I could, beyond blues, beyond rhythm and blues, so I scuffled through some standard chord progressions: "I Got Rhythm," "How High the Moon," "All the Things You Are," and the like. Once in a while it sounded clean and right; other times it was a mess. But each session, I learned something.

Eventually, I formed another group, and talk about a quantum leap. Being the leader allowed me a chance to experiment—nobody could tell me what to play and when to play it. And that's the only way you can learn, is to try and fail. Besides, as the great blind pianist Art Tatum said, "There's no such thing as a wrong note." And Charles Mingus once said, "If you're going to make a fool of yourself, make a *damn* fool of yourself." Sometimes we sounded good, and other times we didn't, but if you heard the first incarnation of the George Benson Quartet, you heard some sincere music. It might not have been the best music you ever heard, but at least it had heart.

Sometimes things were as hard offstage as they were on. The first time I had an out-of-town gig with my own band, it was one of those infamous Pittsburgh winter days, with the wind whipping every which way and the temperature well below zero—the North Pole apparently relocated to Pennsylvania. As I was getting ready to drive to the gig, my stepfather asked me, "Did you put any antifreeze in the car last night?"

I said, "Man, what's antifreeze?" I'd never heard of the stuff.

"*What's antifreeze?*" Tom asked, incredulous. Remember, Tom was a guy who could repair anything—he was an electrician, a plumber, and, as previously noted, a guitar maker—and the fact that I wasn't familiar with antifreeze was probably shocking. "You know what?"

he said. "Don't worry about it. Let me just . . ." And then he put on his winter coat, dragged me out to the car, opened the hood, and peered in. Nodding, he said, "Yeah, the freeze plugs popped. You might've gotten away with it." He paused, then said, "But there's a crack right down the middle of the engine. You darn sure won't get away with *that*."

My heart sunk. I never skipped a gig, *never*. (As of this writing, I've missed less than five shows in my entire career.) "Can you fix it?" I asked.

Smiling, he said, "Course I can." He ran inside and grabbed this new stuff that had just come onto the market—it was called epoxy. Darned if he didn't glue that engine together enough that I was able to drive the car. Granted, it wasn't perfect—it leaked water like crazy, and I couldn't go any faster than 30 mph—but I got to the show in one piece.

Back then, I didn't like the idea of going out on the road, which is ironic, because I've spent well over half of my adult life traveling from city to city, from country to country. But early on, being on the road meant scuffling. Seemed to me that all the cats who came through Pittsburgh, no matter how great they were, never had any money. They showed up in town all raggedy and slouchy, wearing wrinkled clothes and a hungry look on their face. I can't tell you how many times I saw a cat begging a club owner for a draw on his salary.

Speaking of cats coming through Pittsburgh, it was right around then that I met the man who single-handedly—or single-thumbedly, really—changed *everything*. One day I was walking past Pittsburgh's number one jazz club, the Crawford Grill. That night, I had a gig diagonally across the street, over at Mason's Bar and Grill . . . which *wasn't* Pittsburgh's number one, or number two, or even number three jazz club. I peered into the Crawford's window to check out the poster advertising that night's show; there was a picture of a guy who looked like a black cowboy, what with his guitar strapped over his shoulder like a weapon. The cowboy's name: Wes Montgomery.

I thought, *Wait a minute . . . I've heard that name before. That's the cat who doesn't use a pick, and since he doesn't use a pick, he probably sounds like some classical guitarist who plucks with his fingers, like Andrés Segovia.* The poster touted the fact that this Wes Montgomery had won the prestigious *Downbeat* New Star Award, so I thought, *I've gotta check this guy out.*

And I did.

And . . . *wow!*

It wasn't just the way he played the guitar that blew me away—it was the way he *was*. Being in his presence—watching him thumb the strings, hearing him play those magical block chords, listening to him talk with his warm, kind voice—was like attending the most prestigious school in the world. Forget Harvard. Forget Yale. Forget Cambridge. Forget Oxford. I wanted to enroll in Montgomery University, a place where I could earn an undergrad degree in swinging, a masters in chops, and a PhD in hip.

Wes, along with his brothers Buddy and Monk—who respectively played piano and bass, and rounded out his current working band—came into Mason's in between sets, not to check me out, but because the drinks were cheap. After one of my sets, Buddy tapped me on the shoulder, introduced himself, then, without preamble, said, "You know something? You could be a *real* jazz player. You ever think about playing bebop?"

Bebop? Me? Man, I was still trying to figure out what the heck Charlie Parker was doing; the thought of doing it myself was beyond comprehension. I said, "No, Buddy, I could never be no jazz player."

He said, "Man, you *could*. You *absolutely* could. You got the chops."

That was flattering beyond belief. For a minute, I imagined being onstage at a smoky club—a club where the audience listened carefully and clapped politely but raucously after each solo—wearing a sharp suit, backed by a piano/bass/drums rhythm section, maybe a tenor player to my left and a trumpeter to my right, playing a tight arrangement of, say, Bird's "Confirmation" or Diz's "Con Alma," taking two, three, five, ten choruses, never running out of ideas, never stumbling around the fretboard, playing thick chords like Wes and slick single note runs like Grant Green. But then I looked around Mason's and realized that wasn't in the cards . . . yet.

"I don't know, man," I said. "I need some time to get it together."

Buddy nodded. "All right, George. I'll be waiting."

In any event, I realized that if you want to make it as a musician, the road is a necessary evil, so when I was nineteen and was asked to tour with a saxophonist named Willie Love, I couldn't refuse, especially since Willie was one of Pittsburgh's top saxophonists. (Willie, it bears mentioning, came onto the scene around the same time as Stanley Turrentine, another Pittsburgh guy with whom I'd eventually record. My favorite session with Mr. T—and he was called Mr. T long before that other Mr. T—was *Sugar*, an album we cut for the CTI label. To me, that record summed up what Stanley was all about: laid back, groovy, and smart. Willie never garnered the similar acclaim as Stanley, but believe me, that cat could blow.) Again, it was the dead of winter, but since we were in Montreal, the weather was even worse than it was back home. We played two shows, and those were, by far, the meanest gigs of my life.

Canadians, in general, are the nicest people you'll ever meet, but up in Montreal in the early 1960s, well, let's just say that not everybody in the Great White North sipped the milk of human kindness. See, there were gangsters up there, *lots* of gangsters, lots of *nasty* gangsters. They were in cahoots with the club owners and used to charge us bands 10 percent of our salary in order to protect us, telling us, "Yeah, for just ten percent, nobody going to mess with you while you're here." And when they said "nobody," they were referring, of course, to themselves.

Willie, who never wanted any trouble, paid the gangsters without any argument, just like most of the other groups who came through town. But not everybody forked over the money. There was one cat who asked the gangster, "Protect me from what, man?"

The gangster said, "Well, it's just a protection. It's no big deal. It's only ten percent. That's a small price for peace of mind." And then he reached into his pocket, pulled out a pistol, and put it on the table.

He just stared at the gangster and repeated, "Protect me from what, man?"

Word is, they silently stared at each other for a solid minute, and the gangster must've seen something in his eyes that he didn't like, because he said to his partner, "I guess we better get the heck out of here." That guy was one of the very few cats who never paid those thugs.

But that was life on the road, the life of a real musician. Which meant that it was official: I was a real musician.

Interlude #1

A Quick Tour of Pittsburgh

In most any city, jazz cats—the true jazz cats, the cats who want to find their voice and jam and gig and record—will find each other. Sometimes they'll get signed to a big label and become international superstars; sometimes they'll get signed to a small local label and sell a few albums at the mom-and-pop record store in the bad part of town; and sometimes they'll just hang out in the city, playing this or that gig, sidemanning on this or that record. Pittsburgh had its fair share of all of the above.

There were the Turrentine brothers, Stanley and Tommy. (As noted, Stanley became the better known of the two, possibly because he played his tenor louder than Tommy played his trumpet.) Their first big gig was with Max Roach, the cat who, along with Kenny Clarke, all but invented bebop drumming. Max actually wanted to just hire Tommy, but Tommy was a loyal cat and insisted that Max bring Stanley aboard; little did Max know that he was getting one of the greatest saxophone players of all time as part of the package. Their tenure didn't last long, because they both had big troubles with Max. I never heard specifically what those troubles were, but if you didn't want to play alongside the great Roach, those must've been some serious troubles.

And then there was saxophonist Eric Kloss, who was born in nearby Greenville. Now I've heard people say stuff like, "For a blind cat, Eric could play," but you know what? His blindness shouldn't even enter into the equation. That guy could play like nobody's business, and it was little wonder that whenever the great bebop genius Sonny Stitt came through town, he invited Eric to join him onstage. Just before I left Brother Jack McDuff's band, Eric recorded a whole bunch of albums for Prestige, which meant that for a brief while, he and I were labelmates. I always thought we'd play together at some point, but it never happened.

And then there was my main rival, Roger Humphries. Now you'd think that my primary rival would be a guitarist, but not in this case. Roger was a drummer, and a mean one at that. But we came up at the same time, and folks used to argue which one of us was going to be a star: George Benson is gonna be huger than Roger Humphries . . . No, Roger's gonna be huger than George. . . . George . . . Roger . . . George . . . Roger. (See? Rivals!) Roger didn't reach the heights of, say, Philly Joe Jones, Art Taylor, or Tony Williams, but the cat played drums on Horace Silver's Song for My Father, *a classic among classics. Yeah, Roger Humphries did Pittsburgh proud.*

And then there was Spider Rondinelli, a drummer who never made it out of the city. I couldn't tell you why he never went global, because Spider, he could play. Once in the mid-1970s, I saw Spider sit in with Rahsaan Roland Kirk, the blind saxophonist who could play three horns simultaneously, all insanely fast. (Roland used a technique called circular breathing, which enabled him to play continuous lines without a break.) When Spider sat behind the drum kit, Roland—for reasons known only to him, and him alone—decided he wanted to scare Spider off, so he counted off the standard tune "Cherokee" at a faster-than-normal tempo—and "Cherokee" was generally played at a plenty fast tempo to start out with. What

Roland didn't know was that Spider had chops for days, plus he was crazy, so to Spider, "Cherokee" at a million miles an hour was breakfast, lunch, dinner, and two desserts. I don't know how many choruses those cats played, but it was a whole bunch, and Spider never dropped the tempo, and by the end, Roland was sweating like a hog. Maybe nobody took Spider on the road because they were scared he'd show them up.

Now you see why I'm proud as heck to have come from Pittsburgh.

4 Brother Jack

Brother Jack McDuff was a ladies' man. Brother Jack McDuff was a troublemaker. Brother Jack McDuff was a rabble-rouser. Brother Jack McDuff was an imbiber.

Brother Jack McDuff saved my life.

In the early 1960s, McDuff was near the top of the list of heavy cats playing the organ, right alongside Jimmy Smith, Jimmy McGriff, Melvin Rhyne, and Baby Face Willette. He cut a series of records for the Prestige label that were among the best organ-trio sets of the time. Like Jimmy Smith—heck, like most of the big organists of the era—Jack was both a true entertainer and a true musician. He put on a show, but it was always substantial; it wasn't just a cat hitting an endless trill with his right hand and waving to the audience with his left.

When McDuff used a guitar player on a recording session—which was most of the time—it was a good one, for instance Grant Green, Kenny Burrell, or Eddie Diehl. If you were going to share the stage or the studio with Brother Jack, you had to have game, and you had to be at the top of it.

It was 1963, and things were rough for me. I'd been married for just under a year, and we had a newborn son, but it was darn near impossible being a father because I was constantly on the road, and it's hard to pay proper attention to a relationship in Pennsylvania when you're in New Jersey one night, New York the next, and Massachusetts the next. One of my regular stops was Montreal, whose gangster problem had quieted down since my days with Willie Love. I called home and found out that my son was sick: spinal meningitis. I then rang up the hospital and tracked down the doctor. After giving me the prognosis, which wasn't good, he said, "Mr. Benson, listen, we have a new drug we want to try on your boy. We think it'll work."

I said, "Well, why're you still on the phone with me? Why don't you go ahead and try it?"

He said, "We need parental consent. There's nobody here to sign the papers."

"Wait a minute," I said. "My wife's not there?"

"Not as far as I know." He gave an audible sigh. "If we don't give him that drug, by morning, he won't be here. And I can't give it to him without a signature."

After I hung up, I called the airport, hoping against hope to find a flight leaving immediately. "We have nothing going to Pittsburgh from Montreal," the airline's customer service rep said.

"Wait a minute, man," I said, "Are you saying you can't get me home at all?"

"I'm saying I can't get you home *directly*. We can get you a flight with a stop."

"I don't care where I stop. Fly me to England, for all I care. As long as you get me to Pittsburgh before morning."

"Okay, that we can do. We can get you to Pittsburgh via New York." He quoted me the times—they worked. He quoted me the prices— they worked . . . barely. It took all of my money to get back home, but it was worth every cent. I made it to the hospital before the sun came up. After I signed the papers, the doctors gave the boy the drug, which saved his life. He lived for another thirty-something years.

Once it was evident my son was okay, I went looking for my wife. Let's just say that that wasn't a good day. Let's just say I did something I shouldn't have done. Let's just say I got into some trouble, trouble that required me to appear before a judge a few days hence.

The night before the hearing, even though I didn't have a dime to my name, I went out to a club, figuring if I was going to be in prison by the next afternoon, I should have some fun. I was lucky enough to catch Don Gardner and Dee Dee Ford. Don, as mentioned, put in some time with Jimmy Smith, and was now leading a group that had some big hits. (I guess if you were being accurate, they were more *medium* hits than *big* hits. Today, his single "I Need Your Lovin'" is a rare, expensive collectors' item. *Very* expensive.)

The club was all but empty, so in between sets, I wandered over to Don, who I'd met a few times on the circuit. I gave him a sketch of what was going on in my life, then he said, "You know what? Jack McDuff is trying out guitar players. He's looking to replace Eddie Diehl. You should give it a go."

I shook my head. Eddie Diehl was a masterful musician. He wasn't at the level of Kenny Burrell and Grant Green, but the cat could sure play. "I might be going away for a long time," I told Don. "And besides, I can't play that well anyhow. I couldn't make that."

"Yes, you can, George. You *can* make it. You *can* play that gig." That was the kind of cat Don was, positive and supportive of his fellow musicians. "McDuff is gigging at a club on the other side of town. Grab your axe and get on over there."

"Man, I ain't got no money to get out there," I said. "He's on the other side of town."

Suddenly, there was a tap on my shoulder. It was Charles Evans, my natural father. And he'd heard every word Don and I said. "Wait here, George," he said. "I'll be right back."

Sure enough, he returned a few minutes later, huffing and puffing, with a big smile on his face and some silver in his hand, fifty cents to be exact. "Here," he said, handing me the money and panting like an Olympic runner, "take it. You can hop the streetcar, get to the other side of town, and go sit in with that Jack McDuff."

I looked at the money, then my dad, then the money again, then my dad again. "The streetcar is a quarter. There's enough for both of us. So come on, man. Come with me."

He said, "No, you're going to need that other quarter to get back." And that was Charles Evans to a T: you first, him second.

So I went to the other side of town—the bad side of town—all by myself.

Since it was so late, the streetcars weren't coming around that often, so I barely made it to the club before the end of McDuff's last set. When I walked into the club, a few women started screaming, "Oooooh, Little Georgie Benson is here! Little Georgie Benson's in the house! Where's your guitar, Georgie?"

After the next song, Jack, from the stage, hearing the ruckus, called out, "I don't know who the heck this Little Georgie Benson is, but if he wants to sit in and play something with us, he can come on up."

So I went on up, and I played one song, and that was it. Not much of an audition. But I must've done something right, because Jack came right on over and said, "I like what you do. It's a shame you came on the last song of the last night. I'd have liked to hear more." He paused, then said, "Maybe you could bring your guitar down to the hotel tomorrow."

"Where are you staying?" I asked. Turned out he was right down the street from my place in downtown Pittsburgh. I said, "Yeah, I'll be there tomorrow. But it has to be in the morning. I have somewhere to be in the afternoon."

A few short hours later, I knocked on Jack's door. After a minute or two, he opened up, wearing a ratty robe and smoking a big, fat reefer. Truth be told, at the time I didn't know it was reefer, because I didn't know a thing about drugs. I just thought, *Man, that's one funny smelling cigarette.*

He gave me a once-over and—noticing I was carrying my guitar in a shopping bag—grunted, "All right, man. Take your damn guitar out of your damn bag and play me something." (He actually used saltier language than "damn." Considerably saltier.)

So I took my damn guitar out of my damn bag and played him something—some bluesy soul licks, some jazz stuff, whatever I could think of that might impress the cat. Eventually, I hit on a groove that I could tell he loved, so I kept playing it.

Jack's eyes lit up, and he said, "Hold it a minute. Wait a minute. I gotta make a call." He got on the phone and rang up his manager in New York. "Listen, I found this *baaaaad* little young fellow," Jack said. "He's only . . ." Then, to me, he asked, "How old are you now?"

I said, "Nineteen."

Jack shook his head. "He's only nineteen years old. Man, I ain't kidding, this kid is *baaaaad*. I'm bringing him to New York." And then he slammed down the phone.

My head was spinning, and I marveled at how I ended up in McDuff's hotel room: What if I hadn't gone to see Don Gardner? What if my birth father wasn't at the club? What if the streetcar showed up five minutes later than it did, and I missed his last number? What if all those girls hadn't screamed for Little Georgie Benson. Even at nineteen, I realized that the chain of events that got me invited to New York to play with one of the best, most popular organ cats around was amazing. But there was one problem. And it was a big one.

"Hold on, Mr. McDuff," I said. "Just hold on for a second."

He said, "What?"

"I'm going to jail today."

He paused. "What?" he repeated.

"I'm going to jail." And then I told him the story about Montreal and the hospital and the signature.

Nodding, he said, "Will money help you?"

"I really don't know, Mr. McDuff. I really don't know."

"Well, it couldn't hurt." He took a deep puff of his reefer, then scrambled around his room and scrounged up a pile of money: thirty-five dollars. Shoving it into my hand, he said, "I hope this'll help, kid."

"I hope so, too, man."

"Good luck," he said.

"I'll need it." We shook hands, and I hustled off to court.

When I got to the courtroom, I realized that Brother Jack's loan could save my skin. See, my wife thought that I didn't have a cent to my name, because I'd spent all my money getting home from Montreal, and had it not been for that thirty-five dollars, she'd have been exactly right. Had it not been for that thirty-five dollars, I couldn't have afforded court costs or bail or *anything*.

Eventually, the judge called us up, and as I told my side of the story, I could tell by the sour, angry expression on his face he had no sympathy for my situation. Even though my child's life was at stake, I'd roughed up a woman, and even though I didn't hurt her, he did not want to hear that. After I was finished up—and before he could say anything else—I told him, "Your honor, I have an opportunity to leave town. I just got offered a job to play with a traveling band, and you won't see me no more in Pittsburgh after today. He's taking me with him today, if I can get past this."

The judge nodded, then gave my wife a hard look and said, "I don't see any damage on you, ma'am. Why don't you just let him pay the cost of the court? He said he's leaving town. He won't bother you anymore."

She said, "If he can pay the cost of the court, I'll sign the paper." She thought I had empty pockets and would rot in jail.

The judge asked me, "Can you pay the cost of the court, son?"

I said, "How much is it, your honor?"

He said, "Twenty-seven dollars."

Casually, slowly, I reached into my pocket, pulled out my roll, and counted off the exact amount. Before I could hand the money to the clerk, my wife, clearly furious, stormed out of the courtroom without a word.

After she was gone, the judge glared at me. "Now don't go downstairs and jump on her," he said, "because if you do, you're going to prison. I'm telling you right now."

I said, "Don't you worry, Judge. When I said, 'I'm out of here,' I meant, I'm *out of here.*"

That night, I left Pittsburgh a free man, ready to take the jazz world by storm alongside Brother Jack McDuff. My future was brighter than I'd ever imagined possible. I was going to tour the country in high style, and make records that would sell thousands and thousands of copies, and make a name for myself; then cut records of my own; then tour the world, the moon, and mars. Everything was looking up.

That is, until McDuff fired me before our first gig even ended.

Here's the thing: I was an R&B guitar player who knew a little something about jazz, but when I played for Jack in the hotel room, he didn't see that. He just saw a kid who played some hot licks that would sound good in his band and complement his groove. But when we hit the stage that night and he started playing these fast tunes with all these complex chord changes, I was stuck. After the first set, he said, "What's the problem? Why couldn't you hang? Why didn't you play any jazz?"

I said, "Man, I'm not no jazz guitar player. I didn't play any jazz because I can't!"

"Well, now, I didn't know that. So I don't think you're going to be able to make it with this group, George. I've got to let you go."

Now any other day, in any other month, in any other year, I'd have been devastated. Here it was, the first set of my first big-time gig, and I got canned before the end of the night. But I wasn't going to jail, so as far as I was concerned, everything was gonna be okay. I'd figure out the next step when I figured it out.

Jack said, "But I can't leave you in the lurch like that, so I'll take you to New York. You can play with us until then, but when we get there, I've got to let you go. But I think I know of another gig that'll be perfect for you. You know a cat named Willis Jackson?"

I didn't. Jack explained that Willis was a tenor saxophonist out of Florida, with whom he'd recorded a handful of records for Prestige. Willis played with Duke Ellington for a while but was now making it as a soul/jazz saxophonist. Since Willis's music was more blues based than Jack's, he thought we might make a good match.

It sounded great to me, but when I got to New York, Willis had already hired a guitarist, a kid named Pat Martino. Pat, a Philly cat, was younger than me but played twice as much guitar. At that point, I started to get a little nervous—if Pat was representative of the level of musicianship in Manhattan, I was done. After I finished playing those New York gigs with McDuff, I had nothing lined up and nowhere to go, and I didn't think I had enough talent to find steady work.

That night, I played my heart out. I took out all my pain and sadness and fear on that guitar of mine. And I must've done something right, because after the set, Jack's manager ran over, put his hand on my shoulder, and said to Jack, "Brother, did I hear you say you were going to fire this kid?"

"Yeah," Jack said. "Why?"

"You can't fire him," the manager said.

"Why not?"

"Man, you know how much better your band sounds now than when it left here? I suggest we go in the studio and make a record with him. Like, right now."

And that's exactly what we did. And just like that, I was a New Yorker . . . sort of.

As soon as I became an official member of Jack McDuff's traveling circus, one of my cousins invited me to stay with him in his tiny apartment in the city.

I was reluctant. "Man, you'll be crowded out in there," I told him.

He said, "No, George. Come on."

"I don't know, man."

"No, it's cool. Move in."

I sighed, then gave in. "All right, fine, I'll do it. How much money do you need from me?"

"*What*? You're family. I don't want any money from you."

"That's nice," I said, "but I'm going to contribute to your rent."

He finally agreed to take a little bit of bread, and it's a good thing it was only a little bit, because nobody ever got rich gigging with Brother Jack McDuff.

The fact is, I was barely home anyhow because Jack lived on the road. The group went all over the place, all the time: up and down the East Coast, all across the Chitlin' Circuit, around and around the Midwest, then back again, then repeat. For the next two and a half years, my cousin's place wasn't my home as much as it was my base. The only time I was there for more than a day or two was when we played in, say, Newark, Trenton, or New York itself.

Newark has a bad reputation, but it holds a special place in my heart, because in 1963, it was where I cut my first album with McDuff. Newark crowds loved Brother Jack—we always drew big responses and got bigger applause—so the fine folks at his record label decided to cut a live album, in order to capture the rowdy vibe of his Jersey fans. The Front Room would've been the ideal place to do so. The Front Room—which was located on 46 Broadway Street (it's amazing the little things you remember)—didn't have the reputation of the Village Vanguard or Birdland, but it managed to book the baddest cats of the day: Miles Davis, John Coltrane, Art Blakey and the Jazz Messengers, and so on. They closed shop in the mid-1960s, and today, it's a carpet shop. Seems to me that New Jersey would make better use of a jazz club than it would a carpet place.

So that first album was recorded for the Prestige label, for whom Jack had been recording since 1960. It was called *Live at the Front Room*, but here's the thing: It wasn't recorded at the Front Room.

Maybe in terms of setup, the club wasn't a good place to set up the recording equipment. Maybe the acoustics were funky. Maybe somebody didn't pay somebody else off. But something wasn't working, so instead of bringing a portable studio to the Front Room, we brought the Front Room to us. All the club's regulars were invited to the studio and told to whoop and holler as if they were at the club—and I can't say whether or not they were drinking the same thing they'd drink at the Front Room, but that record sounds as live as any live record you'll hear. Thanks to them, the groove was alive—the groove was real. And if there was one thing the 1963 version of the Brother Jack McDuff Quartet could do, it was groove. Our drummer, Joe Dukes: *Groover.* Our tenor sax player, Red Holloway: *Groover.* Brother Jack: *Groover.* And I'd been known to do a bit of grooving myself.

One of the tunes on the album, a McDuff-penned blues song with an interlude called "Rock Candy," became a bit of a hit on the radio and in the jukeboxes. I didn't name the tune, but I'll take some credit for the title: The first time I went to Jack's apartment over on Lenox Avenue in Harlem, his wife said hello, then put a big old dish of rock candy on the table, then left the room to go about her business. Now I've been known to indulge in a sweet or two, so, well, I indulged. By the time she came back to the room, the candy was long gone.

Staring at the empty dish, she asked, "Now what happened to the candy I just put out there?"

McDuff said, "George ate it up."

And thus, "Rock Candy."

Joe Dukes played a mean shuffle beat on "Rock Candy," but most everything that guy played was mean. When Dukes was on that bandstand, he was the knockout cat of the night. McDuff was a showman par excellence, but it seemed like folks in the crowd couldn't take their eyes off of our little drummer. And no matter what city we were in, the musicians came in droves, just to hear Joe—it seemed like *no* drummer passed up the chance to check him out. One night, we were gigging at a place in Philadelphia, a tiny little club located in the basement; I can't even guarantee it had a name. Count Basie's band was playing down the street at a classy joint called Pep's. We went on late, so they liked to come see us after their last show. And good old

Bill Basie, the Count himself, always sat himself right in front of Joe's kit and watched that crazy kid hit the drums backwards and play a roll on the bass drum. He was like thunder and lightning, that Joe Dukes. Yeah, he would swing all night.

A great player, underappreciated in the annals of music, but man, what a nuisance.

Early on in my tenure, Joe got into the habit of berating me about my playing: "You don't know what you're doing," he'd say time and again, in a nasty little tone. And sometimes Joe was right—I still didn't know how to read music, so I couldn't really argue with him—but that didn't make his diatribes feel any better.

Jack had all these wonderful arrangements; he'd come up with passages to make standard 12-bar blues feel less standard—a hip unison riff in between solos here, an unexpected three-part harmony there. The arrangements weren't perfect—let's say that Brother Jack McDuff wasn't Duke Ellington—but they were exciting, and some of the parts were quite sophisticated . . . so sophisticated that I didn't understand them. Now just because I couldn't understand them didn't mean I couldn't play them. Usually I'd be able to figure out a part just by listening to Jack or Red, so my lack of reading ability wasn't always an issue. Joe, however, took it personally that I had to learn the music by ear rather than by sight. Red, on the other hand, was nothing but encouraging. "I envy you," he once said, "because sometimes it takes me three days to learn these parts, and I read music. You, man, in twenty minutes, you got your part down." For instance, on the album *The Concert McDuff*, we recorded an arrangement of "Four Brothers," a song that Woody Herman's orchestra made famous way back in the early days of bebop, 1947. It was a feature for four of the baddest sax cats of the era: Stan Getz, Zoot Sims, Herbie Steward, and Serge Chaloff. (Having four heavies like that in one band just doesn't happen anymore.) Over the years, it became a standard tune, but not too many smaller groups played it because it didn't work without the rich harmonies only four saxophones could deliver. But that didn't stop McDuff. He liked the tune, and he wanted to play it, and we were going to play it—and he was going to make it work—come hell or high water. Jack put together a slick arrangement that had Red playing the lead harmony, me playing the second, and him playing the third. Red read the music, but he still scuffled through the tune, especially when we took it at the tempo Jack wanted, which was *fast*. Me, I just played it like it was nothing, even though I had little idea what I was actually playing. "I don't know how you do it," Red told me. "You're a good guitar player now, but you're going to be a monster someday. Don't pay no attention to what Dukes is talking about."

Joe and I didn't just argue over music: We fought about women, and not just once in a while—it was *constant*. And he was always the instigator, because before I joined the band, he got *all* the women.

Whenever he saw me chatting up a girl, he'd pull me aside and say something like, "Man, that's *mine* you got with you."

"Your *what*?"

"My woman."

"You don't even know her, man," I'd say. "You haven't even spoken to her." I especially enjoyed telling him, "You can't take them *all* home with you *every* night." He didn't care for that one.

After one show down south, he came to my room well after midnight, banged on my door—*boom boom boom boom boom*—and said, "Open up, you nig! You're in there with my girl! If you don't open that door, next time I see you, I'm gonna beat all the black off of you!"

That cat had a serious case of the crazies, and on any given day, he'd make me angrier than I'd ever been, and angrier than I ever would be. I wanted to kill that little guy every day because he was so cruel to me, always making a fuss about something. Pretty much the only time I didn't wish him ill was at the end of our sets, when he took his solo. What that cat did on the traps was incredible, magical, indescribable. But the rest of the time, he picked on me, and I swore that when the time and circumstances were right, I was going to beat him up and put an end to the madness. Turned out, I never got a chance to do anything like that, and it turned out that that was a good thing.

One afternoon, when we were on our way to a gig in his hometown of Memphis, Joe, in a rare moment of contemplativeness, told me a nice story about how he and his family regularly went to Beale Street to hear Elvis Presley. When he finished the tale, he got all quiet for a second, then said, "I haven't been home in six years." After another pause, he said, "I haven't seen my mother in six years. Six years, George! How could I let that happen?"

When we hit town, he took me to his house, and the second his mother laid eyes on her son, she started bawling her eyes out. Right then, it dawned on me that no matter how much you might hate somebody, someone somewhere loves that person, and if that person is loved, they have some good in them. And he was such a magnificent drummer that there were times I thought he was one of the greatest things that ever happened to mankind.

Slowly but surely, my guitar playing improved, and Joe took notice, so in 1964, when he was given the opportunity to cut his own album, much to my surprise, he hired me. (Actually, he hired the entire band—the record was called *The Soulful Drums of Joe Dukes with the Brother Jack McDuff Quartet*—thus, there's the possibility that the Prestige Records folks made him use the whole band, so he was stuck with me whether he wanted me or not.) *Soulful Drums* is the only record that demonstrates what Dukes could really do, and if you're a drummer, or you appreciate some good percussion work, you owe it to yourself to track it down.

Dukes was (and is) remembered as a greasy drummer—one of the best cuts on his album is even called "Greasy Drums"—but when you listened a bit deeper, you realized that he was more than backbeats and blues: The cat was soaked in jazz history. As was the case with so many drummers of the era, Joe's hero was Pittsburgh's own Art Blakey, and I didn't realize it at the time, but Joe wore his Blakey influence on his sleeve. For instance, Joe liked to play what's called a single-stroke roll, which is difficult to describe but easy to identify. In the wrong hands, it's a show-offy move, but he was so musical about the whole thing that it felt natural, not fake. (Side note: I didn't truly learn what Blakey and his band, the Jazz Messengers, were about until Joe hipped me to what I was missing. Thanks to Joe's constant pestering, I checked out Blakey's shows whenever I could, and since the Jazz Messengers worked as much as the Jack McDuff Quartet, we often ended up in the same city. And man, those bandmates of his were something else, a Who's Who of modern jazz: Wayne Shorter, Lee Morgan, Cedar Walton, Curtis Fuller, Bobby Timmons—heavy cat after heavy cat after heavy cat. All of the band's arrangements were classy, and there was never a bar that went by that wasn't exciting. Until he died in 1990, Art took his Jazz Messengers all over the world, always giving his best, never phoning it in. It was little wonder that he, along with Duke Ellington, was jazz's greatest ambassador of the era, and I'm proud that Art became and remained my friend until the end.)

Dukes wasn't the only cat in the band who regularly claimed he would do me bodily harm because I wasn't doing the music justice; our esteemed leader made his fair share of threats, threats that were inevitably made on the bandstand. If Brother Jack had just the right (or wrong) amount of booze or weed, and I played something he deemed to be wrong, he'd grab the microphone and cuss me out using the filthiest, rawest words you can imagine.

Finally, after a particularly nasty rant, I snapped: "If y'all don't lay off, I'm gonna take y'all outside and beat y'all old men up! I'm nineteen years old! Y'all can't take me! We're going out in the alley, right now!" McDuff and Dukes just stared at me for a second, then they both pulled out switchblades. But that didn't stop me: "I don't care! Y'all don't scare me! Bring your switchblades into the alley! I'll beat y'all up anyhow!" Fortunately, cooler heads prevailed: Nobody went out into the alley, and nobody got beaten up. But it got them off my back.

In retrospect, I'm glad they stayed *on* my back; granted, their methods were barbaric, but for the most part, it was about making me a better musician so we'd be a better band. And there was so much incredible stuff happening in the early and mid-sixties that you *had* to be better than the best. You had Miles Davis breaking in what ultimately became his second classic rhythm section: Herbie Hancock, Ron Carter, and Tony Williams, and even though those cats had only been together for a few months, they were communicating telepathically to the point that it sounded like they'd shared the stage for decades. And then you had John Coltrane sounding equally telepathic on *A Love Supreme* with McCoy Tyner, Jimmy Garrison, and Elvin Jones. And then you had all those cats who were recording for Blue Note Records: Lee Morgan, Hank Mobley, Lou Donaldson, Jimmy Smith, and on and on and on. If you were going to survive, you had to compete, and if you were going to compete, you needed your entire band firing on all cylinders, whether you were playing bebop, hard bop, avant-garde, or your good old garden-variety blues. They wanted the best for me because they wanted the best for themselves, and I couldn't blame them. Sure, they could've been a bit nicer about it . . .

But thanks to their encouragement (and insults), I started going to clubs regularly to check out the competition, and when I went, I didn't merely hang out: I *listened*, really and truly listened. I heard Thelonious Monk playing all these jagged lines, at once funky, mathematical, and childlike. I heard Bill Evans paint beautiful pastel pictures with the keyboard. I heard all my fellow guitarists—Grant Green, Kenny Burrell, Barney Kessel—playing lines and chords that were miles above and beyond what I was doing. And I did my best to absorb.

Eventually, I was able to incorporate some of what I heard into my own playing, and that impressed Jack, partly because he was glad to see me grow as a musician, but mostly because I made him and his band sound better. If you listen to some of my later recordings with the band—*Silk and Soul* from 1964 and *Hot Barbeque* from 1965, for instance—man, I'm kicking it behind Jack . . . *skak ba b'doo k'chunk k'chunk*, and so on. I filled in the blanks and accentuated what needed to be accented. We were a machine, a well-oiled machine.

One problem: My solos weren't too good. Maybe mediocre. At best.

But I was feeling boxed in, because McDuff was hung up on the blues. Some of our tunes were slow, and some were fast; some were minor key, and some were major key; some were funky, and some were straight-ahead bebop, but virtually everything was blues based. Now I love the blues as much as the next person, but sometimes a cat needs a break.

One night after a set in which we played nothing but that I–IV–I–V–IV–I form, I asked Jack, "Man, does every song have to be the blues? What happened to all the pretty music?"

He stared at me silently for a bit, then, in a surprisingly calm, rational tone, said, "George, blues is accepted everywhere in the world. You could be in China and play the blues, and they'll like it."

"Yeah, but I don't want to play blues all—"

He cut me off. "Oscar Peterson plays blues in *everything*. Everything he plays is bluesy. That's why the cat is so popular all over the world. Hell, they love the blues out there in China." (I've come to find out that that was one thing Brother Jack McDuff was absolutely right about: Chinese music fans can't get enough of the blues.)

So I started listening to different records in a different way. I went back to my Charlie Parker sides, and, like Oscar Peterson, almost everything he played was *full* of blues, even all that pretty stuff on *Bird with Strings*. Even "Laura," the prettiest song on the record, is lightly coated in barbeque sauce. Miles Davis's *Kind of Blue* is the epitome of blues, even though there's only one 12-bar tune on the album, that being "Freddie Freeloader." (It's worth mentioning that

I cut a version of "Freddie Freeloader" on a Jon Hendricks record with Bobby McFerrin and my great friend Al Jarreau.) Even Coltrane at his most atonal was channeling the spirit. Darned if Brother Jack wasn't right. I thought, *You know what? This cat might know what he's talking about. I should start paying closer attention.* From that point on, when McDuff talked about music, I listened.

He wanted me to learn how to build my solos from the bottom up. "First of all, George, you've got to get into a groove, to get into the rhythm. That'll get the audience with you. They'll be on your side. That's when you show them some technique. You play some hot licks every now and then, just to let them know you can play. But then go back to playing those blues. Groove, rhythm, hot licks, blues. That's the formula."

So I gave it a shot. I'd hit a groove, and the people went, "Mmm hmm." Then I'd throw in a bit of rhythm, and the people went, "Yeah, that's right." Then I'd play eight or twelve bars of fast lines, and the people went, "Go George, go!" Then I'd finish it up with a blues lick, and the people went, "Yeeeeeaaaaaaaaaahhhhhhhhhhh!" It got the crowd stirred up, and that was terrific, but I have to admit that I went along with it reluctantly at times, because there was a part of me that was frustrated I didn't have the chance to play like Hank Garland.

Jack's hero was the great Jimmy Smith, of course. Jimmy was flashy and funky and always bluesy, and he cut fabulous record after fabulous record. One of McDuff's favorites was from 1962, called *Bashin': The Unpredictable Jimmy Smith.* (That title was on point—Smith had been known for his periodic unpredictability.) The terrific, thoughtful saxophonist/arranger/composer Oliver Nelson did all the arrangements, the hippest of which was "Walk on the Wild Side," a bump-and-grind tune that had Jimmy bashing the organ over what sounded like an entire orchestra of horns.

The record was a success with both critics and listeners, and Jack decided to do something similar, so he enlisted one of the greatest arrangers of the era and cut *The Brother Jack McDuff Quartet with the Big Band of Benny Golson.* Now Benny, who'd cut his teeth with my fellow Pittsburgher Art Blakey, wasn't the kind of guy who'd show up to a session with some tunes he slapped together the previous night. He took his time and wrote and arranged to the best of his abilities, and man, those abilities were *something*—complex, dense, and nonstandard.

For a guy like me—a guy who didn't read music—that was a problem. Jack knew I didn't read, but he insisted on using me on the date anyhow, assuming I'd figure it out. After arriving at the studio and setting up my gear, I peered at Benny's chart and mumbled, "Oh, man." I had no idea what I was going to do. Fake it? Hide behind my amplifier? Pretend I had a stomachache? Fortunately, Benny decided to run through all the tunes twice before we started recording, and that's all I needed. Once I committed it all to memory, I got cocky: "All right, y'all, let's make this record! Come on, come on! Let's do this, Jack!" Turned out to be one of the highlights of my young musical life, and it gave me a taste for playing with a big band, something to which I'd indulge in the years to come. (Several years later, I heard one of the album's cuts on the radio. I dug what I was playing, but I thought, *Man, I was trying to sound sophisticated. I should've done what Jack told me to do: Play some more blues.*)

My most memorable musical moment in McDuff's band was strictly an accident. It was on a tune of his called "Blues 1 & 8" from another live album called *Brother Jack at the Jazz Workshop Live!* The song's title referred to the tune's form: The whole band played one chorus of blues, then the first eight bars of the next chorus, after which, *boom*, everybody dropped out except for the soloist, who then had four unaccompanied bars to do his thing, to fill that open hole with whatever he wanted, be it a single note, a trill, or a Dizzy Gillespie lick. And the solos got passed from one cat to the next: Jack threw it to me, then I threw it to Red, then Red threw it back to Jack. By the time we got to my third time around, I couldn't think of anything special to play. See, Jack and Red were doing all this funky, bluesy stuff that had the crowd screaming, and I couldn't figure out how to keep up that crazy energy.

Now, I don't know where this thing came from. I'd never played this thing before. I'd never even *thought* about playing this thing before. And *this thing* was the sound of a chicken. And it's impossible to tell you how to do it in writing. Guess I'll have to sit down and show you sometime.

For the year and a half after that record came out, everyplace we went—and when I say "everyplace," I mean *every*place—some cat would come up to me and beg, "Play that song with the chicken in it, man. *Play that song with the chicken in it!*" And most of the time, I did. And it blew my mind that one gimmick—one little different thing, one unexpected moment—changed everything. Folks now recognized me as George Benson, guitarist, rather than George Benson, Jack McDuff's guitarist. I guess if you play something with heart, soul, honesty, originality, and integrity—without sacrificing innate musicality—you might be more memorable than if you play material for the hipsters, the critics, and your bandmates. And believe me, I filed away that golden nugget of information for later use.

All of a sudden, I was a viable entity, so much so that the fine folks at Prestige Records wanted me to cut an album of my own. But just to play it safe—just to make sure my built-in audience joined me on the journey—Prestige president Bob Weinstock and the session's producer, Lew Futterman, insisted that McDuff, Holloway, and Dukes join me in the studio. Since we'd developed a level of communication over our dozens and dozens of live gigs—and since everybody had been keeping their switchblades to themselves—I agreed.

Some of the album's up-tempo numbers—"Shadow Dancers," "Rock-A-Bye," and especially "My Three Sons"—could've come right out of a McDuff session, but what I believe differentiated it from Brother Jack's records was the fact that I played pretty. "Easy Living" was the first sweet ballad I'd ever committed to wax, and it was so lovely that McDuff stepped away from the organ and sat down at the acoustic piano, one of the rare times he was heard on vinyl without his Hammond B-3.

We called the album *The New Boss Guitar of George Benson*, and a lot of folks considered that to be somewhat egotistical, but the fact of the matter was that it wasn't about me being the boss of the guitar. See, I'd bought myself a new guitar, and it was big, it was expensive, and it was, in the parlance of the day, *boss*. The title was literally an homage to my new axe. Besides, I'd never refer to myself as the boss of the guitar. That title belonged to Wes Montgomery. He was the boss right up until he passed away—and even beyond.

Meanwhile, Brother Jack McDuff's traveling circus continued blazing a trail across the United States, seeing the sights, swinging the stages, and gigging at all the fine (and not-so-fine) clubs in the country, one of the finest being the Jazz Workshop in San Francisco. The Workshop was everything you'd want in a jazz club: The stage was lower to the ground than that of, say, the Village Vanguard, so the audiences could see us sweat; the small, round tables—many of which were topped with a colorful flower graphic—came right on up to each other, which added to the intimacy; and the crowds were California cool, always dressed to the nines, always hip to our records.

One night, who should wander in but Buddy Montgomery. Naturally, I recognized him right away, and much to my surprise and delight, he recognized me . . . sort of.

In between sets, he wandered over, scrunched up his face in confusion, and asked, "You look familiar, man. *Really* familiar. Where do I know you from?"

I said, "I met you in Pittsburgh. You and your brothers were playing at Crawford's, and my band was playing across the street at Mason's, and you used to come by because the drinks were cheaper, and you told me . . ."

He snapped his fingers, gave me a huge smile, and said, "You're that kid that was playing, the one that I told he could play bebop. Man, I *told* you that you could play jazz. I was right."

I stared at Buddy, unable to say a word, completely blown away. As I tried to compose myself, I thought, *Wes Montgomery's brother told me I can play. I guess I made it. I'm big-time.*

Buddy was a great cat, and we became friends almost immediately. (That sometimes happens with other musicians. If you communicate well on a musical level, you communicate well on a personal level.) Naturally, he introduced me to Wes, who soon became more than a friend: He was my mentor, my inspiration.

One of the reasons Wes liked me so much was that I would never criticize him about anything. I mean, who was I to question a titan like that? The only thing I'd done to that point was travel the country with wild cats like McDuff and Dukes, and cut a handful of records that showed I could play some decent blues and a nice ballad or two. Wes showed an entire generation that there was a different way of looking at an instrument; he was the first guy since Charlie Christian to make such crucial stylistic and technical leaps. And those records he did for Riverside: his debut *Fingerpickin'*, which featured him wailing some of Buddy's slick tunes, including the classic "Bock to Bock" . . . *The Wes Montgomery Trio*, an organ trio set that was slicker than slick . . . *Full House*, a live set with Johnny Griffin tearing it up on tenor sax, backed by Miles Davis's current rhythm section of Wynton Kelly, Paul Chambers, and Jimmy Cobb, and featuring the definitive version of his most popular composition, "S.O.S." George Benson was not about to question anything Wes Montgomery did, said, or played.

He told me some wonderful things about life and music, Wes Montgomery did, personal things—things about being a man, things about being a musician, things about other musicians, things that I haven't shared with anybody and never will. But while his advice and experience was vital in my development as a person, it was more about being in his presence. Wes taught me how to balance honesty with tact; he never criticized people to their face, but he would tell me his honest opinion in a manner that was constructive rather than hurtful, and because his views were expressed articulately and with gravitas and intelligence, I ended up agreeing with him on a lot of things.

The funny thing is that I rarely solicited his advice on how to play my instrument. Early on in our relationship—soon after we met—I asked him, "Could you show me something on the guitar?" I didn't ask for anything specific. I just wanted *something*.

Wes said, "No, I can't show anybody anything." He wasn't being mean or flip. Just honest.

I said, "Really? You can't show me *anything*? Why not?"

He gave me a small grin and said, "I'm too busy learning myself."

At the time, I had no idea what he was talking about. How could the cat who made *Bags Meets Wes!*—his brilliant album with the Modern Jazz Quartet's vibraphonist Milt Jackson—have anything left to learn? That album was darn near perfect, as are most of his other recordings. But years later, after I'd toured the world many times over, cut a dozen or so albums of my own, and been a sideman on dozens more, I understood what he was talking about. I didn't know everything, not by a long shot, and I never would. When you play jazz—actually, when you play *any* musical style—there's always something to learn about feel and time; about swinging and grooving; about playing above your intelligence, engaging the crowd, and being a mature professional. I'll keep absorbing new information until I pack up my guitar for good . . . and then I'll learn some more.

One night I was gigging at a club—where and with whom, I don't recall—and I was *on*, man, wailing away like there was no tomorrow, handling a way-up-tempo song in a confident, smooth manner that frankly surprised me. Now in those days, when I performed live, I almost always sat on a stool, and when things were going particularly well, I'd shut my eyes tight. Near the end of my solo, I did something either really right or really wrong, because I heard somebody yell, "George! George! What're you doing? What're you doing?"

I opened my eyes, and there was Wes, giving me that Wes look, a look that tried to convey some message or another, a message that, in the moment, I couldn't figure out at all. Man, I was so freaked out that I almost fell off that stool. And I don't mean that in a metaphorical sense. I literally almost fell off the stool and onto my backside. But somehow, some way, I managed to keep my composure and finish the solo with a flourish. Wes gave me a slight grin and a little nod, so I must've done something right.

I spread the Montgomery gospel at every given opportunity, and most everybody whom I hipped to about Wes agreed that he was the baddest cat out there. One dissenting voice: my stepfather.

"Man," Tom told me after I explained to him what Wes could do, "there ain't no other guitar player out there who can touch Charlie Christian. He was the best of the best, and that's the end of that."

I couldn't believe it. "Have you ever heard Wes Montgomery play? Those chords? Those chops? That thumb?"

He shrugged. "I heard him. He's all right. He's just okay."

If there's one thing Wes wasn't, it was "just okay." I asked, "Are you *sure* you heard Wes Montgomery play?"

"I heard him," he repeated in a tone that made it clear he didn't want to discuss the matter any further.

One day not too long thereafter, I was back in Pittsburgh, visiting family and resting up before a gig the following week. I found out that Wes was playing at Lawson's in Harrisburg, so I drove my stepfather the 198 miles, just so he could see what he needed to see. We arrived to the club in the middle of a set, and there was Wes, on the bandstand, tearing that joint up. My stepfather looked around nervously, knocked out by the crowd's enthusiastic response. I imagined what was going through his head: *Man, Charlie Christian couldn't get an audience all lathered up like this.* He didn't say a word for the rest of the set and for a few minutes afterwards. Finally, I said, "So?"

He nodded. "Yeah. He can play." That was high praise from Tom Collier.

"That's right, man," I said, clapping him on the shoulder. "He can play." It was a nice moment.

McDuff's crew gigged at the Jazz Workshop a whole bunch, but then again, we gigged everywhere a whole bunch, and by "everywhere," I mean *everywhere*, including, much to my surprise and joy, Europe. In 1964 I made my first trip across the ocean, where I met a bunch of native cats who were doing things I'd never heard, one of whom was a French violinist by the name of Jean-Luc Ponty. Jean and I were both twenty, and both musicians, so we clicked right away. We were in Sweden, and both of our bands were preparing to appear on a local television show. After watching him tear it up during rehearsal, I cornered him and said, "Jean, show me something."

"Show you what?" he asked.

"Something!"

"Something?"

"That's some great stuff you play," I said. "There's one line you play, it goes down and sounds like this . . ." And then I sang it for him.

He nodded. "Oh, yeah, that's a C double diminished scale."

I said, "Okay, double diminished. Teach me *that.*" So Jean ran it down: C–Db–Eb–E–Gb–G–A–Bb–C. And that one scale—that one little uncommon, off-center scale—opened up my eyes to a whole new world. It was one of the most important musical lessons I'd ever had. "That's beautiful, man. If I could play two bars of that on violin, I'd be a happy man."

"You can do it, George. Go out and buy a violin."

"Naw, man," I said. "I played a little back in the day, but now I'm still trying to learn guitar."

"Violin will help with your guitar playing."

"I don't know, Jean."

"It *will*."

"I don't know, man."

This went on for who knows how much longer, until I promised him that I'd get myself a violin when I returned to the States. And I did. Turned out, Jean was right. Revisiting the violin made me a better guitarist. I guess the more instruments you know, the better you'll be.

Fast-forward to the winter of 1984. It was well after midnight, and I'd been asleep for hours, and would've stayed that way had the phone not rang. I grabbed it and mumbled, "H'lo."

"*Bonjour, Monsieur Benson. Comment allez-vous?*"

"Jean! What's up, man?"

"I'm in New York, cutting a record. Can you come down to the studio?"

I peered at the clock. "It's after one."

"We're going to be here *alllllll* night," he said. "Come on down. I just need you for this one song."

I owed Jean-Luc a great debt—that double diminished scale was *huge*—and I loved the guy, so I couldn't refuse, and I'm glad I didn't. We played this song he called "Modern-Day Blues," and it went to the moon. More than one person has told me, "George, that's the best record you ever made."

Jack McDuff worked constantly, to the tune of forty-eight weeks a year, and that set the tone for the rest of my career. I used to tour as often as I possibly could, even when I was exhausted beyond belief, and even when I didn't necessarily need to. Even today, if my datebook is empty—if I don't have some gigs or recording sessions on the docket—I get antsy. And, as previously noted, I've skipped on less than five gigs in my life. I mention that for the second time because it's something of which I'm particularly proud. My attitude has always been, *If somebody wants to see George Benson, they're going to see George Benson.*

But despite our full calendars and the fuller clubs, the Jack McDuff Quartet didn't make any money. I was young and naive, so I never understood how it was that we played most every night but never took in much cash.

I was the only cat in the band who had a little bit of money in his pocket, primarily because I had no vices. While I made sure that I stayed financially afloat, the other guys—especially Mr. Joe Dukes—spent all their money on libations. There were plenty of times Joe got so desperate that he was forced to borrow money from me. I obliged, but because he was such a nuisance, I charged him interest, to the tune of 6 percent. And man, Joe hated me on payday.

After McDuff would hand us our salary, I'd pull Joe aside and ask, "Man, where's my $31.80, Joe?"

"I borrowed thirty," he'd whisper under his breath, clearly not wanting McDuff to know he'd dug himself into yet another hole.

"Listen, man, don't play with my money," I'd say. "Six percent interest. Give me my bread."

He'd glare at me, then say, "You jive, Benson. Here's your damn money." That happened time and again. Thanks to Joe Dukes, I probably ended up earning an extra month's salary each year.

Since I had a few extra bucks, I decided to treat myself to a portable black-and-white television. (We rarely stayed at hotels that offered TVs, but that's what happens when you don't spend more than eighteen dollars per week for a room.) The guys in the band, having spent all of their money on whiskey, wine, and women, knew they'd never be able to afford a television of their own, so they got jealous. One day, while we were setting up for a gig, McDuff said—in front of the group—"Benson, you got about as much right to a television as a monkey does to a wristwatch," then went on to explain why he deserved a television of his own.

I said, "Man, if you want a TV, why don't you go buy one? You make more money than me."

So he did.

Now, my television was a little portable thing made out of plastic, but that wasn't good enough for Brother Jack McDuff. He bought himself a real television, the kind of television you'd see in somebody's living room, and that thing weighed 150 pounds. This cat was so competitive that he hauled that thing all over the country, just to show me up. He used to tell me, "Mine's better than yours, man. You got black and white. I got color."

For all his faults, Jack was an independent man, never one to impose on anybody—for instance, I don't remember him ever asking for help carrying that crazy color television of his. Seems like the only time he consistently accepted aid from somebody was if they told him they thought they could score him a bag of reefer, especially if the bag was big. As volatile as it was working with Jack, I owed him a debt of gratitude. Had it not been for him, I could've been either rotting away in jail or stuck in Pittsburgh, leading Little Georgie Benson and His Bank Robbers—so I tried to help him at every given opportunity.

To his credit, whenever Brother Jack got into trouble—and trouble usually meant getting busted with reefer—he always took his punishment like a man. It seemed that no matter what state he was driving through, the police stopped him on the turnpike, and when the officer strolled over to the car, Jack opened the window, took a big hit off of his pot pipe, and blew a puff right into the cop's face.

"What's in that thing you've got there?" they'd ask, knowing full well what McDuff was sucking. "And what's the pouch on the windshield?" Inevitably, he'd shrug and take another toke, at which point, the cop would say, "Get out of the car and put your hands behind your back." And then, once again, three-quarters of the Brother Jack McDuff Quartet would go to the local police station to negotiate their leader's release.

(I never understood the appeal of marijuana. One day I asked Jack if I could bum a cigarette, and he stuck a reefer in my mouth. I took a drag, then said, "Wait a minute. What's this?"

Grinning from ear to ear, he said, "That's a reefer."

I took it out of my mouth, and naively said, "That's what a reefer looks like? This little thing here?"

Still smiling, Jack said, "Yeah. How you feel?"

"How am I supposed to feel?" I asked. "*What* am I supposed to feel?"

He blinked. "You don't feel nothing?"

"No, nothing. How much does this stuff cost?"

He said, "Fifty cents?"

"*Fifty cents?*" I said. "For *this*? Man, that would've gotten me two packs of Kools." And that's the reason why I don't do drugs. To me, spending half a buck on forty cigarettes was a much better investment than spending it on one joint. That's something else for which I owe Brother Jack.)

I was even there for Jack long after I left his band.

It was the late 1980s, and I'd just finished a gig in, I believe, New Jersey. After the show, one of the local promoters tugged at my elbow and said, "Hey, George, Jack McDuff got arrested on the turnpike. They got him down at the station."

I thought, *Again?* Then, without a second's hesitation, I said, "Where's the police house?" After the promoter gave me directions, I jumped in my limousine and told my driver to step on it. When we arrived at the station, I immediately got into a fight with the cops. (And please note that by "fight" I mean shouting, not hitting. I'd stopped hitting decades before. Besides, when you have great lawyers like mine, violence isn't necessary.) Eventually, one of them pointed to a hard plastic chair in the corner and said, "Just sit down right there. We'll bring your friend down in about fifteen minutes."

Forty-five minutes later, I got one of the cop's attention. "Brother, I've been sitting here for almost an hour. Your partner told me he'd be back in fifteen minutes."

"Cool it, pal," the cop sneered. "He'll get here when he gets here."

I stood up. "I'll be back here in fifteen minutes with a lawyer." When I told him the attorney's name, he turned white and said, "I'll have your friend down in five minutes. If you pay the fine, you can take him with you."

"Man, it'd be my pleasure." And it *was* my pleasure. See, there's nothing Jack could have asked me that I wouldn't have done. But he didn't beg *nobody* for *nothing*.

In 1976, soon after my album *Breezin'* came out and took off, I ran into Jack. After pleasantries, he told me, "That song 'This Masquerade,' man, what I like about it is that it wasn't a negro hit. It was an *everybody* hit. It was a *worldwide* hit." When I was with the band, Jack rarely said anything kind about my playing—he was on my back constantly, as noted—so it knocked me out when he said he was proud of me.

For most of us jazz cats, no matter how wonderful a sideman situation may be, you can't stay forever. You get hungry for either a new challenge or a band of your own, so sooner or later, you have to move on. Miles Davis eventually left Charlie Parker's group. John Coltrane eventually left Miles Davis's group. McCoy Tyner eventually left John Coltrane's group. If those cats could leave those other cats, then I could leave McDuff.

The end began in Los Angeles. During a break in touring, I went to L.A. to visit a girlfriend. Soon after I hit town, I ran into one of those three-card monte guys on a street corner in West Hollywood. (For those of you who aren't hip to card games, three-card monte is one of the oldest scams in the book. The dealer—aka the con man— lays out three playing cards in a row. He then picks up one of the cards and tells his mark, "Follow this one." Then he'll move them round and round and round, and you have to identify your card. When he does the sample, he makes it easy to figure out which card is yours, so the second time around—when he asks you to lay down some money and place a bet—you're confident you can pick the card, no problem. The thing is, that second time around, the dealer will use all kinds of sleight of hand and misdirection to confuse you, and it's almost impossible to pick the correct card.) This cat, man, he was *slick*, and ten minutes later, all my money was in his pocket, and I was broke. My only possession was my new boss guitar, a guitar that had cost me almost $1,000.

In order to afford a plane ticket home, I had to pawn that boss axe of mine. The most I could get for it was $75. I went to the bus depot and bought a ticket—it cost $72, which left me with $3, and I had to make that three bucks last two and a half days. Even way back then, even in the mid-1960s, you couldn't eat on three bucks for one day, let alone two-plus days. I didn't starve, but it was close.

That night, in order to keep my mind off my numerous troubles— and to avoid any card hustlers—I scoured the streets in search of a club that would let me in without having to pay a cover charge. Finally, I found a place by the water whose owner took pity on a broke jazz musician. I settled in at the bar and got a gander at the pianist, and man, that cat sounded *gooooood*, a lot of Oscar Peterson and a little bit of Bud Powell. I asked the bartender the pianist's name. "It's Freddie Gambrell," he said. "He recorded with Chico Hamilton, the drummer, about seven years ago. And dig this: He also plays a mean bass and a meaner trumpet." He gave me an appraising look, then added, "And guitar. Not as good as you, but still pretty good."

"Thanks," I said, somewhat glad to be recognized. A small compliment and some tiny acknowledgment of my lot in life briefly made me forget my empty pockets.

"And you know what else?" he asked. "The cat is blind."

"*What?*"

"Yeah, man. Completely blind. Just like Art Tatum."

It dawned on me that Oscar Peterson's main influence was Art Tatum, so I wondered if Freddie's style was an unconscious (or conscious) nod to his fellow blind keyboardist. Either way, Freddie was an inspiration, so much so that after his set, I introduced myself. "Hey, man, you sure sound good. I'm George Benson."

We shook hands, then he asked, "You're the guitar player with Jack McDuff, right?"

"That's me." Recognized two times in one night! That felt pretty good.

"I've heard you. You're a *baaaaad* cat. Go get your guitar. Come play something with me next set."

My heart sank. "I don't have it with me." The last thing I wanted to do was tell this guy I had to pawn my axe.

"That's cool. You can use mine. It's in the dressing room."

He brought me up on the third tune, then called out a song I'd never heard. Before he counted the tune off, I leaned over and mumbled, "I don't know that one, Freddie."

"It's all right. I'll call out the changes. First chord is a C with a flat five over a D9. One, two, one two three four."

That meant that Freddie would be playing a C-major chord in which the G—which is the fifth note of the scale, C–D–E–F–G—was taken down a half step, so that it would be a G-flat, a sound that is at once discordant and hip. (If you want to know what a flat five sounds like, listen to any Charlie Parker or Dizzy Gillespie record. Bird and Diz played them all the time, and they laid on them *hard*.) A D9 means a D-major scale with the ninth note played on top, the ninth note being E. Not hard, but not easy.

Naturally, it was an up-tempo tune, not as fast as, say, Clifford Brown's version of "Cherokee," but speedy enough that I had to do some serious scuffling. By the time I played the C with the flat five over the D9, he was on to something else. And then, he did the most embarrassing thing one musician could do to another: He stopped the song. "You know, George," he said, "you didn't . . ."

"You said a D9, man!"

He said, "Yeah, but I didn't mean *that* D9."

"A D9 is a D9!"

He said, "No, no, no, no, no. There're lots of ways you can do it. You can do it this way." Then he played a chord so pretty that it made your heart sing. "Or you can substitute it with this." And then he played another chord that wasn't pretty so much as funky.

"Oh. Man, that's interesting." I stared at Freddie's hands on the keyboard, forgetting that I was on a stage, in front of an audience of paying customers. Freddie must've forgotten, too, because he said, "Did you know you can do this here? Or this? Or this?" These lessons, while painful, were almost as crucial to my development as those delivered to me by Jean-Luc Ponty.

I finally made it out of California, and when I returned home, even though I was bone tired, I didn't sleep for two nights because I couldn't stop working on all those substitute chords that Freddie Gambrell hipped me to. Now Jack McDuff and Red Holloway were good players—no, *great* players—but they were blues and soul cats. Sure, they could play some good bebop, but they weren't as complex as the true bebop cats. And they most definitely didn't play Cs with flat fives over D9s. Freddie opened up a whole new world for me, and I was so excited that I played all night. And man, it was a blast.

My neighbor, however, didn't appreciate it.

At 3:00 a.m.: *Bang bang bang bang bang!* It sounded like somebody was hitting my door with a sledgehammer. "Benson, cut out that racket! If you don't turn that down, I'm busting down your damn door!"

Without missing a beat, I yelled, "Man, if you come in here, I swear I'm gonna wrap this guitar around your head!" I must've scared him *bad*, because I never heard another peep out of the guy. But I did turn down my amp. A little.

Being one-fourth of the Brother Jack McDuff Quartet was a life-altering experience. I learned how to be a professional—to give my best every night, even if I'm exhausted, and even if there are only three people in the room. I learned how to handle, shall we say, *personalities*, to deal with cats who pull switchblades and threaten to stab you in the middle of a set. I learned how and when to play the blues, and how and when to play pretty, and how and when *not* to play. But it wasn't until then that I learned that if I added some complex, hip, slick chords to my arsenal, I'd have the confidence to start my own band.

Interlude #2

Catching the Early Trane

I would argue that Pennsylvania—what with all the cats who came out of Pittsburgh and Philadelphia—is one of the three or four most jazz-centric states in the country. Pittsburgh's contribution to jazz history has been discussed, so let's talk about Philly, a place that some folks call the City of Brotherly Shove. The list of native Philadelphians who made marks on the music world is outrageous: We're talking the Heath Brothers (saxophonist Jimmy, bassist Percy, and drummer Tootie; there must've been fairy dust in the Heath household); we're talking Charlie Parker's late-career trumpeter/right-hand man Red Rodney; we're talking Ray Bryant and Bobby Timmons, the two funkiest acoustic pianists of their (or any) generation.

But the two best-known Philly jazz cats are saxophonists John Coltrane and Benny Golson. Benny and I have crossed paths many, many, times, and man, that guy has stories, and was always happy to share them. One of his favorites was that of when Trane encountered a man who changed his life and, by proxy, everybody else's.

In the early 1950s, when they were twentysomethings learning their way around the saxophone, Benny and Trane hung out constantly, partly because they enjoyed each other's company, and partly because they wanted to see what kind of new stuff the other had come up with over the previous twenty-four hours. Benny was a dyed-in-the-wool bebopper-in-training, while Trane was, for the most part, a rootin'-tootin' saxophone player—an R&B player who, at gigs, walked up and down the bar, playing one note over and over again in order to get the crowd hyped. Matter of fact, his nickname was Johnny One Note.

One day word got out that the baddest cat in the world was coming to Philly for a gig at a local music hall: Charlie Parker. Benny and Trane made the gig, and like most people who heard Bird on a night when he wasn't too inebriated, they were properly blown away.

For weeks after the show, Benny couldn't get in touch with John, which scared him a bit, because, as noted, they saw each other every day, and twice on Sunday. When Benny finally tracked down his friend, Trane was a totally different cat in every way imaginable: his demeanor, his level of maturity, and, of course, his saxophone playing. He was no longer Johnny One Note—he was Johnny One Hundred Notes. (When he released Giant Steps some fifteen years later, he was Johnny One Thousand _Fast_ Notes.) All because he spent an hour in the presence of Charlie Parker.

There's a lesson there: When you hear something that touches you, learn it, absorb it, then make it your own. The number of Wes Montgomery solos I've listened to over the past fifty years can't be counted, so he's in my DNA—and my fingers, for that matter—but even when I'm not covering one of his tunes, Wes is along for the ride and will offer directions on the best route to complete my journey, but I'm always behind the wheel. And if you're a jazz cat, that's the way it should be. You can't live in a vacuum. Take the past to heart, then take it to the future. That's how you keep the music alive.

5 Discovered

Brother Jack McDuff always had beautiful music pouring out of his Hammond B-3, and we did things that no other organ group of the time could touch. But I was hearing a different sound in my head, something trickier and less bluesy, something that Charlie Parker might dig. So I went back to Pittsburgh and, for three months, played at a dive called the Rendezvous Lounge, accompanied by only an upright bass and drums. There weren't too many cats playing with a guitar/bass/drums trio—usually there was a piano or a horn thrown in there for good measure—but the sparse instrumentation allowed me the freedom to experiment and find my own voice. And since it was my group, and the Rendezvous wasn't a high-pressure gig, my solos could go on all night, and I learned to play chords and licks I'd never before imagined. This gave me the confidence to take the next step: starting my own *real* band.

The thing was, in the mid-1960s, it wasn't easy for a musician who played straight-ahead jazz to get steady work. (Heck, it wasn't easy in the early 1960s or the late 1960s, the early 1970s or the late 1970s, or the . . . well, you get the point.) So you'd think that few musicians, given an opportunity to join a band that had a bit of potential, would pass it up. But when you're a young guy with only one solo record to his name and no guaranteed gigs, it wasn't easy to get established cats to join up.

Fortunately, I remembered this cat I'd met in New York, a young organist from outside of Buffalo named Lonnie Smith. He dug McDuff and used to come hear us on a regular basis. One night he cornered me and said, "George, whenever you get ready to start a band, just call me," then slipped me his phone number. I didn't know whether or not he could play the Hammond, but he was enthusiastic and knowledgeable, so I gave him a ring. "Lonnie," I said, "I'm getting my own band together, and I want you to . . ."

Before I could even finish the sentence, he said, "I'm in. But I'm stuck here in Lackawanna, and I don't have a car."

"Awww, man, I don't have a car either. Let me see what I can do."

I asked around, and this girl I knew helped me track down an old, raggedy automobile, which I bought for a nickel. I found an even more raggedy trailer, hitched it up to the car, then went up to rescue Lonnie.

After Lonnie got settled, I called up a friend of mine—Mr. Jimmy Boyd, another cat who'd expressed interest in helping me launch my solo career. I told him about Lonnie, then asked, "Can you get us any work?"

I could almost hear him smiling over the phone. "Yeah, man. I think I got something for you. Not too far from Harlem."

"Minton's Playhouse?" I asked, excited beyond belief. I mean, that's where Bird and Diz and Monk and Charlie Christian—*Charlie Christian, man!*—and all those old bebop cats got their starts.

"No, George. Not Minton's." He then named a club of which I'd never heard. "It's *near* Harlem, not *in* Harlem. It's actually in the Bronx," he said.

"I ain't never heard of no jazz clubs in the Bronx."

"It's not a jazz club," he said.

"Not a jazz club? So what kind of club is it, then?"

"They'll pay you," he said. "Do you care?"

"Well, since you put it that way . . ."

So for the next few weeks, Lonnie and I played behind a revolving cast of go-go girls, and believe me, for those few weeks, my blues training came in handy. See, dancing girls don't care about flatted fifths or diminished ninths. They want to shake their stuff, and be-bop doesn't make for quality stuff-shaking music.

Finally, right when I was getting fed up with playing variation after variation of "Night Train," Jimmy called with another gig, this one at a club in Manhattan called the Palm Café. The Palm was right on 125th Street, and from the outside, it looked like a little hole in the wall, but when you went in, you were guided into a giant room with a great sound and a great vibe. We were right down the street from the Apollo, and the cats who gigged there regularly dropped by the Palm, most notably the Hardest Working Man in Show Business, Mr. Star Time, Soul Brother Number One, the Godfather of Soul himself, James Brown.

Lonnie and I, we knew all of his tunes, and if we didn't know it, we could fake the heck out of it; that sort of funky jazz (or jazzy funk) was candy to us, especially Lonnie, who'd been playing James's music for years. He was a hero to us all, so when he asked me one night, "What's your name, son?" I nearly spit out my drink.

"George, sir. George Benson." I called him "sir" because he had a reputation for being a tough guy. Sure, I could handle myself if something broke out, but why take that chance?

He gave me an appraising look, then said, "How'd you like to work with the James Brown band? You know what I'm saying? What did you say your name is? George, George, George, George. You want to work with the James Brown band?"

Now *that* would've been a fun gig—this was 1966, right when he was riding the wave of "I Feel Good" and "It's a Man's Man's Man's World," and his popularity was over the moon. His fans were raucous, and each show was an event with a capital *E*. But would it have made sense for either my career or my musical growth? I'd just moved on from a blues-based gig in order to expand my horizons. It was a tough call. Without consulting my brain, my mouth said, "You know, Mr. Brown, we're jazz musicians. We want to play some jazz stuff. I'm flattered and honored, but I'll have to take a pass."

James stared at me for almost a full minute, nodded, and walked away. (Do I regret not becoming one of the Famous Flames? I don't know, man. Can you imagine what that would've sounded like? *Mmm, mmm, mmm.*)

Here's the funny thing about the Palm Café gig: About halfway through our residency, I learned that the Palm's owner hated jazz music, just *hated* it. Actually, he didn't hate it so much as he didn't *get* it—I don't think he would've known a jazz song if it walked up to him on the street, stuck out its hand, and said, "Hi there, I'm 'Freddie Freeloader' by Miles Davis, the second cut on side one of *Kind of Blue*, which is one of the greatest jazz albums of all time. Nice to meet you." When I found that out, my first thought was, *This fool is gonna fire me.* But my second thought was, *If he doesn't know what jazz is, then he doesn't know what jazz is, and there's nothing I can do.* However, I thought I'd be able to use his ignorance to my advantage.

When we started swinging particularly hard, the cat would come up to me after the set and ask, "Is that jazz? Because I don't want no jazz in here."

I'd say, "No, man, this ain't no jazz."

Whenever he'd ask, "Well, what is it, then?"

I'd point to the other side of the club and tell him, "My cousin's over there. Gotta run."

We weren't allowed to play jazz for the entire night anyhow, because the last twenty minutes of each set was set aside for the go-go girl. (No matter how hard we tried, we couldn't escape those go-go girls.) Toward the end of what was to be our last gig at the Palm, I noticed a Caucasian guy strolling into the club. Now, that wasn't completely unheard of—we'd attract a Caucasian cat every now and then—but this guy stood out. He had a classy, expensive vibe about him, which was compounded by his date for the night, an immaculate woman covered in diamonds and rubies, with a beautiful hairdo. This couple clearly wasn't there to hear somebody play a shuffle blues while a half-naked girl grinded away, so I ended the tune and told the dancer, "We're done! Get off the stage! Get down, get down!"

After she was gone, I turned to Lonnie and said, "'Clockwise!' One, two, one two three four." "Clockwise" was an original tune of mine, a blues with an introduction and interlude that consisted more or less entirely of flatted fifths. As written, it was a fast tune, but I was so hyped that I counted it off even faster.

The cat didn't sit down for the entire song. When we hit that final note, he clapped harder than anyone I'd ever seen at the Palm.

When I got off the stage, he motioned me over and, before he even introduced himself, took a pen from his pocket and a napkin from the table, then he held out both and said, "Just sign your name here. This is a contract with Columbia Records. Just sign your name right here."

Jimmy Boyd came from nowhere, grabbed my hand, and said, "George, don't sign that. Man, you can't sign that."

I said, "Why not? This is Columbia Records, man."

He said, "Ain't nothing on there. They could put *anything* on there."

"Oh, man. You know, that makes sense." (This is why Jimmy was my manager for the next eleven years.)

The cat from Columbia said, "Okay, okay, okay, just come down to my office. We'll work all this out." He gave me his card, then stuck out his hand and said, "My name is John Hammond. I look forward to sitting down with you."

After he split, Jimmy said, "John Hammond! Wow! John Hammond! Man! John Hammond!"

"That name sounds familiar," I said. "Where do I know him from?"

Jimmy explained that John was one of the greatest record producers and talent scouts in the history of modern music. "He found

Billie Holiday and Count Basie and Big Joe Turner and Teddy Wilson and Benny Goodman and—are you ready for this?—Charlie Christian." He paused, then said, "And now it looks like he found you."

Talk about an out-of-nowhere surprise. When I brought Lonnie on board, I had no idea that we'd garner interest from one of the biggest, if not *the* biggest, record labels in the world. I knew we sounded good, but there were dozens of cats who sounded as good, if not better, who were recording for large independent labels like Prestige, Contemporary, and Blue Note—heck, even Wes Montgomery did most of his work for Riverside. And here I was, the former Little Georgie Benson, getting offered a contract that would put me on a roster alongside the likes of Duke Ellington and Miles Davis. It was humbling, it was thrilling, and it was inspiring. I hoped I could deliver music that would be worthy of Columbia Records, that would reward John Hammond's faith in me.

The only problem was that Columbia, understandably, didn't want a guitar/organ duo, so I had to put together a full band, and quick. Thanks to my tenure with Brother Jack, I'd become comfortable playing alongside organ, drums, and saxophone, so I brought in a drummer from Kansas City named Jimmy Lovelace, and man, Jimmy could burn on bebop, swing, blues, *everything*; he'd also briefly shared the stage with Wes Montgomery, and if Wes thought he was good enough, then you can believe I thought he was good enough. And while I dug what Red Holloway was doing on tenor, I wanted a different sound, so I hired a young cat named Ronnie Cuber, whom I met while McDuff was working opposite Ronnie's then employer, trumpeter Maynard Ferguson. While Ronnie could handle every kind of saxophone under the sun, he was a terrific baritone player. When Ronnie, Lonnie, and I played something in unison, and I took the high part, Lonnie the middle, and Ronnie the bottom, man, that was something that nobody had ever heard.

Before they finalized the contract, the Columbia people wanted us to go into the studio on their dime and do what they called a tape audition, which was exactly what you'd think it was: us playing a bunch of songs that would be given to the Columbia brass, who would then give us a yes or a no. We must've been doing something right, because right after the first tune, Hammond burst into the studio and yelled, "This is no longer a tape audition! This is a recording session!"

Oh, man.

As much as I wanted to cut an entire album of jazz tunes like "Clockwork," I realized that people knew me for my blues-based work with McDuff, so it made sense to do some groove-oriented material, like our cover of "Ain't That Peculiar," which had been a hit for Marvin Gaye the year before. The reasoning was that if somebody wanted to buy a George Benson record, there should be something on there that reminds them of the George Benson they knew from three years before. And in order to attract a wider audience—and a different audience—John and I decided it would be a good idea for me to sneak in a couple of vocal tunes, so we reached into the George Gershwin songbook, and I cut what I hoped were swinging renditions of "Summertime" and "A Foggy Day."

Did the record—which was titled *It's Uptown with the George Benson Quartet*—sell more copies due to the soul covers and vocal cuts? We'll never know, but it brings up a topic that I've discussed time and time again: balancing musicianship and commerciality.

There are a lot of great jazz writers out there, cats supportive of the music, who analyze it in a manner meant to inform and attract readers and listeners. They'll approach a record or a concert with open ears and no preconceptions, letting the music and the moment dictate their take. Then there are other critics to whom jazz means one thing and one thing only: straight-ahead. And by "straight-ahead," I mean bebop or swing or Dixieland. If there's a backbeat, they're far less interested. Me, I've always felt that stylistic labels aren't fair, that every song, every album, every concert, should be judged on its own merit. So what if it doesn't sound like the artist's previous record? So what if you were expecting to hear one thing but got something else entirely. So what if the musician chooses to make music for many rather than a few? If the few doesn't care for it, they don't have to buy it . . . and they don't have to disparage the artist for trying something different, something unique, something that doesn't meet their expectations. I'm sure there were some folks who bought my Columbia debut and were surprised that I sang those Gershwin songs. I'm sure some of them wanted me to "play that song with the chicken in it," but I wanted to stretch and to grow—to dig deep into my roots and let the world know that I was more than a bluesy jazz cat.

John Hammond was a terrific partner in crime because, like me, he felt that if the music was good, the style didn't matter, that if the song was good and performed with sincerity, listeners would get on board eventually—and, more often than not, he was right on target. What with his track record, if anybody could speak with authority on how things worked in the music business, it was him—but at the time, I didn't realize just how important of a figure he was.

After one of those early sessions, John and I fell into a conversation about one of his signees, Bob Dylan. Now I didn't know who Bob was—and, much to my detriment, I wasn't particularly interested in learning—so I stopped listening to him. Realizing he didn't have my full attention, John launched into a story about some cats he knew I'd want to hear about.

Back in jazz's early days, arguably the four most important cities for the music's development were New York, New Orleans, Chicago, and Kansas City. John was riding through the Midwest, and just when he got past Kansas City, he heard a tune on the radio that grabbed his ear so hard that he turned right around and drove back, so hot was he to find that band. He toddled around the city, asking people where the radio station was; when he got the address, he went down to the studio and asked everybody in the building who the heck that bandleader was. He was told it was Bennie Moten, so he did some more detective work; then, when he found Bennie, he offered to pay to bring him and his band back to New York. Sadly, Bennie died before he got out of K.C., so John asked the band's piano player, Bill Basie, if he'd like to take over. Bill said yes, and the rest is history. It was that easy. John also explained that Bill Basie became Count Basie because since jazz already had a Duke—that being Edward Kennedy Ellington—it needed a Count. Not only did the cat know music, but he knew marketing.

I never dared to dream something like this could ever happen, that a kid from the ghettos of Pittsburgh with only a few years of jazz experience and one solo record under his belt would be compared to the great Charlie Christian—a god among guitar players—by the man who'd discovered Charlie. So once I understood what John Hammond was really about, I hung on every word the man said. It got to the point that sitting in a room with him meant everything to me.

What I didn't realize—and what he didn't tell me, much to his credit—was that he was having some issues with the Columbia brass, who didn't want to add a little-known guitar player to their roster, because they didn't think I'd make them any money—plus they'd had a guitar player several years before who hadn't made them any bread. In 1961, Columbia signed Kenny Burrell, who, as previously noted, was one of the finest guitarists of our era, but the head honchos didn't see him as a star, so they wouldn't let John offer him a contract unless Kenny sang at least one song per album. Now Kenny had a nice enough voice, but he wasn't a vocalist, and John knew that, but John wanted him so badly that he agreed to the vocal stipulation. And that was exactly what happened with my contract. It turned out that John didn't just *want* me to sing; I *had* to sing. But you know what? I loved those vocal tracks—still do—and they helped start me on a journey that I might not have otherwise taken. So let's just say it was meant to be.

The label was in such financial disarray that the brass even discussed letting John go, something that, considering what he meant to the company—not to mention his vital role in music history—was shocking. Their attitude was, *What has he done for us lately? This guy's not making us any money, so let's get rid of him.* Columbia was such a mess that somebody somewhere mistakenly sent him his notice, and John darn near had a heart attack. But they kept him around for almost another ten years, during which time he discovered Bruce Springsteen.

John cared about his acts, a trait that wasn't necessarily common among A&R cats—too often, these guys only show up to your concerts if your product is doing good numbers, but John, if he had the time, he'd come by. He even trekked up to Harlem to see me at Minton's Playhouse, and if John was a good storyteller, Teddy Hill, Minton's owner, was *great*.

Teddy was quite a character, man, what with his omnipresent cigar, sharp wit, and remarkable memory, always ready to talk about the history of jazz. There were the classic tales, like the one about how John Birks Gillespie became Dizzy Gillespie—how he was always showing up late to rehearsal, making jokes the entire time, and Teddy was frustrated to the point that one day he said, "Where's that dizzy trumpet player?" And then there were the lesser-known incidents . . .

"One day I was coming out of my office," Teddy told me after a late-night set, "which was catty-corner from the bathroom. A guy came out of the bathroom, stuck a pistol in my nose, backed me up into the office, tied me to a chair, pulled out a Band-Aid, and taped my mouth shut. Then he got right up in my face and said, '*What's the combination to the safe?*'

"I said, 'Mmmmmmmmmmmmmm.' That's all I could say, because I had a damn Band-Aid over my mouth! But I survived. Because that's what you do in my world, George. You survive."

Thanks to Teddy and his tales of the bygone bebop era, whenever I set foot in Minton's, I pictured Bird and Diz and Monk inventing a whole new style of music. Imagine that: Those cats took a little bit of this and a little bit of that, put it in a blender, and changed the world as we knew it. They were the elite musicians of the time—of all time—and they grew up there, they fought there, they created there, they got addicted to drugs there, they did *everything* there. And being part of that lineage, even a small part, was both unexpected and thrilling. (Probably the greatest thrill was when Teddy told me, "You remind me of Charlie Christian. Yeah, I remember when he first came through here. He was just like you." I loved hearing that stuff. But can you blame me? Who wouldn't?)

Those were some long nights there at Minton's. Most evenings, we went on at ten and didn't finish until four in the morning, and there were many nights (and mornings) when John Hammond was with us from beginning to end.

There weren't too many race problems, but you didn't see too many Caucasians up around 210 W. 118th Street. "Man," I once asked John, "aren't you afraid to come up here?"

He said, "No, George. I've been coming up here a long time. I've never had any problems in Harlem."

"But this is a different crowd here at Minton's," I pointed out.

"Oh, nobody's going to bother me."

And sure enough, nobody ever bothered him . . . but they darn sure bothered me. Every night, the neighborhood thugs stole my hubcaps, then sold them back to me after the last set for two dollars apiece.

Minton's was twenty years removed from its bebop heyday, but it was still a proving ground for young musicians, because if you could make that crowd happy, then you had a good chance of making the jazz world happy. (Every night, for hour after hour, we scuffled hard to do just that.) We saw all the newcomers come through, one of whom was a very young cat named Chick Corea. Chick, who was playing piano with the great tenor saxophonist Stan Getz, used to come by every Monday night when he wasn't gigging with Getz, and he tore that place *up*. You could almost feel the buzz. And then there was Monty Alexander, a pianist from Jamaica who somehow managed to weave his native island grooves into the sounds of modern bebop.

I wanted to try out some of the downtown clubs, like the Village Gate and the Village Vanguard, because, man, those were some good jobs. But here's the thing about the Vanguard: Yes, it's one of the most famous clubs in all of jazz history; yes, all the greats played there; and yes, there have been some classic recordings cut on that stage (the sound of the room is so distinct that most cats can tell if an album was recorded there within a few bars): Sonny Rollins's *A Night at the Village Vanguard*, the Cannonball Adderley Sextet's *In New York*, John Coltrane's *Impressions*, the Bobby Timmons Trio's *In Person*, and on, and on, and on. But it's *tiny*. The ceiling is low, the stage is cramped, and the drinks are small. They say it seats 123 people, but I think that's a generous number. But it's the Vanguard, and if you're a true cat, that's where you want to be.

I wanted to be a true cat. I wanted to be there. The problem was, I couldn't get out of Harlem because we hadn't nailed down a true identity. Miles, Coltrane, Getz, those cats had a thing, and ours was still developing. Eventually, I managed to get a gig as an opener for my Columbia label mate, the great Thelonious Monk.

Monk had a reputation for, shall we say, eccentricity, and he was a big fellow, about six feet three, probably 250 pounds, so at first, frankly, I was a bit scared of him. I didn't think he'd beat me up or anything, but this was a guy who almost got into a fist fight with Miles Davis during a recording session, and if you were willing to mix it up with Miles—who had trained with professional boxers—who knew what you would do?

It turned out that Monk was the definition of a gentle giant, a vulnerable teddy bear of a man who just wanted to make music and be liked. I dug sitting with him in the Vanguard's cramped kitchen and listening to him talk about his early days in New York. ("I was only seventeen years old," he once told me, "and I scared everybody

With Tom Collier at the infamous Little Paris Night Club in Pittsburgh, 1950

At home in Pittsburgh, 1952

*All photos courtesy of the
Benson Family Archives
unless otherwise noted.*

With Tom and my mother, 1953

An autographed photo to my then manager, Eugene Landy, 1953

With my manager
Harry Tepper, 1953

Making noise with Tom Collier, 1954

Performing at a Pittsburgh sock hop, presided over by disc jockey Merri Dee, 1954

The Altairs, 1960; I'm on the lower right, holding my homemade guitar

On drums,
1960

Publicity still, 1963

An ad for a 1965 bill featuring the Brother Jack McDuff Quartet

Columbia Records publicity shot, 1967

With Earl Klugh, 1969

Solo, 1971

Solo, 1973

Solo, 1973

With Phil Upchurch, 1974

Paying tribute to Benny Goodman with, among others, vibraphonist Red Norvo and vocalist Helen Humes, 1975

With Arif Mardin, 1975

With Tommy LiPuma at the 1977 Grammy Awards, celebrating *Breezin'*

Collecting a gold record
with my manager Dennis
Turner (center, holding
record) and others, 1977

With Earl Klugh and
Chet Atkins, 1979

With Ella Fitzgerald, 1980

With Quincy Jones and Stevie Wonder, 1980

With Wynton Marsalis, 1980

Celebrating *Give Me the Night* going gold at 3300 Warner Boulevard in Burbank, 1981; that's my Cousin Reggie, hiding in the back

With John Hammond Jr., 1985

Live in Pittsburgh, with Jorge Dalto, Dennis Davis, Michael O'Neill, and Stanley Banks, 1986

On tour (as usual), 1991

With B.B. King,
1995

With Bill Cosby,
1999

With Brother Jack McDuff, 1999

My first Nat King Cole tribute concert, Walt Disney Concert Hall, Los Angeles, 2012

Rotterdam, 2013 (Photo credit: Thom Hall)

Playing with
Verve . . . and
Miles . . . and A&M

There are a whole lot of different kinds of personalities in the music world—artistic temperament, and all that. Some folks are consummate professionals, while some folks make life difficult for others. Some folks are open minded and are willing to experiment, while others forge a path from which they never diverge. Some folks are all about the business, while others are all about the art—and in both cases, it's sometimes to their detriment. Me, I don't like drama. All I do is play my guitar and sing a few songs, because that's what I've always done, and that's what I'll always do. I don't get caught up in whose record has sold more copies, or who did this first, or who plays better than this guy, that guy, or the other guy. I leave all that other stuff up to everybody else—the writers, the fans, the other cats. But no matter how hard you try to avoid the ugliness, it sometimes feels like everywhere you turn, somebody is scrutinizing your every move, and when that happens, well, things can get uncomfortable, awkward, and flat-out strange.

My second record for Columbia, *The George Benson Cookbook*, made a little bit of noise, sold a few copies, and garnered me more notoriety than I'd ever had. I didn't see it coming—I think the only people who did were John Hammond and that cool guitar player I met in Italy—so I wasn't prepared for the backlash. For that matter, I had no idea there'd be backlash. Since jazz wasn't as popular as rock 'n' roll, I assumed the community—critics, fans, musicians—would support their peers in good times and in bad. I didn't expect attitude, but I got it—and, man, what a shock.

It got to the point where every lick I played was scrutinized. If I played a blues lick—something out of my McDuff-era bag of tricks—somebody would say, "Aw, you ain't nothing but a corny blues-guitar player." If I played a rock lick—a style with which I'd been experimenting—I'd hear, "You ain't nothing but a flashy rock player, man. Playing all that rock 'n' roll, all the damn time." If I played a soul lick—something in a Motown or Stax groove—I'd hear, "You ain't nothing but a commercial soul guy trying to sell records and tickets."

I refused to get into the discussion, because it wouldn't do anybody any good if I argued with a paying customer, a journalist, or the saxophonist from down the street, but I can't lie: Sometimes it hurt. *What does it matter what kind of lick I'm playing?* I'd think. *I ain't no Andrés Segovia, and I ain't even trying to be Andrés Segovia. I ain't no Billy Butler or Grant Green or Chuck Berry or Charlie Christian or Steve Cropper or Kenny Burrell and I darn sure ain't no Wes Montgomery. I'm just George Benson, and George Benson has absorbed all kinds of music, and it's going to come out in my soloing, whether or not I want it to, because when you improvise, you play what's in your head and heart, and if I've listened to a Beatles' record yesterday, well, I might play a chord that sounds like John Lennon, but the next second, I might play a Barney Kessel lick. I'm the sum of my parts, and that sum is me.*

One night after an encounter with a prickly fan, I remembered something my dad had told me several years before: "Son, whatever you do, put a jazz tune on your album, no matter what."

"Why is that so important?" I said.

"There are people out there who've followed your career since the beginning, and in the beginning, you were a jazz guy. You want to make sure they *come* with you and *stay* with you." Years later, I put out an album that didn't have one jazz guitar lick on it; the second he finished listening to the album, my dad called me up and said, "Don't ever do that again. People love your guitar."

Another surprise was the rockiness of the record industry, but considering how jazz musicians—heck, *all* musicians—had been treated over the years, that shouldn't have come as a shock. Even though *Uptown* and *Cookbook* had sold a respectable number of copies, Columbia started giving Team Benson some problems, especially in terms of promoting. Now, I was aware that the label had to divide its promotional resources equally between its artists, but it felt like we'd been orphaned. The ads for my records were few and far between, and not only did that put a dent in my record sales, but it also hurt the size of our crowds at shows. I mean, how can somebody come to a concert if they don't know about it? It should be noted that John Hammond remained a staunch supporter throughout. He tried to help in every way imaginable, but Columbia was a giant company, and there was only so much he could do. The label still didn't want a guitar player, and despite my vocal tunes, to them I was and always would be, first and foremost, an instrumentalist.

Finally, after weeks of mounting frustration, Jimmy Boyd sat me down and said, "George, we've got to get out of this contract."

"I don't know, man. Is that the best idea?" I was conflicted. On the one hand, they weren't supporting me in a manner that would perpetuate my career, but on the other hand, a contract in the hand is worth two in the bush. "Isn't something better than nothing?"

"Listen, George," Jimmy said, "once word gets out that you're available, people will start calling."

Sure enough, word got out. And sure enough, people started calling . . . with deal offers—offers that were loaded with *real* up-front money—and believe me, it's a rare thing for jazz cats like me to get *real* up-front money. Prestige gave me next to nothing, and Columbia gave me a nice taste, but these new offers were over the moon.

Naturally, Jimmy wanted to move forward, so he hired one of the top music lawyers in New York to get us out from under Columbia's thumb. This lawyer was a feisty kind of guy who was known for his ability to get things done—and man, he liked his reputation. "Ain't nothing I can't do," he boasted during our first meeting. "I can break *any* contract."

When it came to the business side of things, Jimmy did most, if not all, of the talking. But when the lawyer said that with such confidence and bluster, I couldn't help but blurt out, "How?"

"How? Because the guys who make up the contract always leave an out for themselves in it. And there, within *that* out, is *your* out. So there's no such thing as ironclad, because they always leave an out for themselves. So do you guys want out?"

John Hammond was so important to me that I had to think long and hard about moving on. Leaving a man who'd been so supportive, a man who'd taken a chance on a wet-behind-the-ears kid from Pittsburgh, would be heartbreaking. But I had to consider my future. Languishing on a label, no matter how big that label was, would've killed all of our momentum. I'd hustled to get to that point, and I didn't want all my hard work to go to waste. So we set up an arbitration hearing with Columbia Records and filed a grievance with the Musician's Union. Columbia wasn't pleased.

I wasn't privy to the behind-the-scenes machinations—Jimmy kept me out of that stuff so I could focus on music—but things with the label eventually got so contentious that he had to bring me into the loop. "Columbia holds a lot of sway with our lawyer's firm," he explained, "and they know our lawyer is slick, that he's the best, so Columbia is going to lean on the firm to send the guy on vacation, so he won't be here for the arbitration hearing."

"*What?* They can do that?"

"Man, they can do anything they want. They run the town."

"But he's our lawyer!"

"I know," Jimmy said, looking angrier than I'd ever seen him, "but I'm telling you, that's the way it is."

The day before we were to go to court, Jimmy called the lawyer's office to confirm that he'd be at the hearing. Sure enough, the receptionist told Jimmy that the lawyer was on vacation, and not only that, but there apparently wasn't another lawyer available to represent us. So we had to go to the hearing all by ourselves, the humble guitarist and his trusty manager versus the big, bad record label.

On paper, it looked bad, like there was no way we could win . . . but then, about half an hour before the arbitrator entered the room, I recalled something. "Hey, Jimmy," I whispered, "remember what that lawyer cat said about no contract being ironclad?"

"Yeah."

I pointed to his briefcase. "Pull that contract out of there." We went through that thing page by page, and sure enough, there was some language—a phrase—that we were sure would be our out. The second the arbitrator appeared, we read him the line; he shrugged and told the Columbia team, "Sorry, gentlemen." And just like that, I was free to begin the next phase of my career.

After it was all said and done, I got into a deep discussion with John Hammond. "This has been hard on me, George," he said, "*really* hard. I understand why you had to do it, but let me ask you this: *How* did you do it?"

"I don't want to get specific, John," I said, "because I might have to do something like this again. Let's just say that we found an out in the contract, and we walked. But I'll always be indebted to you. You got me a few dollars, you helped me upgrade my life, and you helped me get *out there*. But, man, I learned the hard way that business is business." I paused, then asked, "When you signed us, how many records did you think we'd sell? Rough estimate."

"Somewhere between three thousand and six thousand," he said.

"*What?* Those tunes we put on there, man, when I'm at the clubs, I know there're people digging them. I've seen people enjoy them with my own two eyes. I've heard people applaud them with my own two ears. And besides, there's a hundred eighty million people in America. You mean to tell me that only six thousand of them would want to . . ."

"Listen," he said, "it has nothing to do with you. Even the most famous jazz artists in the world don't move units. Heck, Miles Davis only sells twenty thousand records."

"That doesn't make any sense to me. Somebody's doing something wrong here. I think if you put something on that record that people want to hear, they'll buy it."

"You're probably right, George. You're probably right."

That night I lay in bed, replaying the conversation, and thought about how I could make a difference, how I could help people realize the beauty and artistry of the musical style that had set up shop in my head, my heart, and my soul. I decided then and there that no matter what, I was going to put something on my records that I thought everybody would want to hear, and not worry about the fallout. And if anybody wanted to discuss it, I'd point out that Louis Armstrong was not a fan of the song "Hello Dolly," but if you saw him perform the hoary old tune, you'd never guess that, because every lyric fell out of his mouth like he wrote it. With every word, he made you believe that that song meant the world to him. Despite his disdain, it remained in his repertoire until the very end, probably because he realized that if somebody came to his show strictly to hear "Hello Dolly," they'd also hear "Basin Street Blues," "West End Blues," "St. Louis Blues," "Weather Bird," and "St. James Infirmary," and maybe they'd learn a thing or two about the stuff that he really cared about, then spread the word and perpetuate the music.

And then there was Stan Getz. Up until 1961, Stan was a cat who straddled swing and bop, and had developed a loyal following among fans and critics because his style was smart and accessible. But I guess his fan base, no matter how loyal, wasn't particularly big, so he discovered the bossa nova, did up some samba records, brought Astrud Gilberto into the studio, and *bang*, he was an international superstar. And all he did was what I wanted to do: Put something on his record that he thought everybody would want to hear, and something that he also felt good about.

Now all I had to do was figure out what that something was. Turned out that that something was a new label.

To some, switching from Columbia Records—the biggest label in the world—to Verve Records—the second or third biggest *jazz* label in the world—was a less-than-wise career move. But Verve, man, they had some special stuff going on.

When I connected with them, they'd been around for just over two decades, and in that time, the company, founded by Norman Granz—one of the greatest, if not *the* greatest, businessman in jazz history—had cemented its place in music with its dozens and dozens of classic records from cats like Oscar Peterson, Dizzy Gillespie, Johnny Hodges, Lester Young, Buddy Rich, and Lionel Hampton. Not only that, but it also re-released material that Granz had put out on his earlier labels, Norgran and Clef, and dig this roster: Charlie Parker, Ella Fitzgerald, Count Basie, Art Tatum . . . *wow!* And, unlike Columbia, they weren't afraid to have multiple guitar players on the label: I'd be joining the likes of Tal Farlow, Barney Kessel, Kenny Burrell, and Grant Green . . . not to mention Wes Montgomery.

After five or so years with Riverside, Wes signed with Verve in 1964, and even though the albums he cut for Riverside were some of the best jazz guitar playing you'll ever hear, they didn't sell all that well, but the less-than-stellar numbers certainly had nothing to do with the records' quality and diversity. For example, in terms of his instrumentation on these albums, they ran the gamut from guitar/organ/drums trios, to a piano/bass/drums/congas rhythm section, to a bebop-style quintet, to a session with strings. The material was good ol' straight-ahead jazz: some bebop chestnuts, a whole lot of standards, and some slick originals (I don't think Wes ever got his proper due as a composer; the cat could *write*: "D-Natural Blues," "Four on Six," and "S.O.S." were darn near classics). But I would guess that Riverside didn't have the means to distribute, market, and promote them on a large scale, so they probably sold somewhere between three thousand and six thousand, just like John Hammond said—enough to perpetuate Wes's career but not enough to take him to the next level.

Verve, however, had more muscle, so they were able to get Wes *out there*, and they knew that if they were going to put him *out there*, they had to put him *out there* with material that would appeal to both his core audience and casual jazz fans.

Enter Creed Taylor.

Creed Taylor was a listener, and I don't mean just when it came to music. A quiet cat with a heavy presence, he paid close attention to what was going on around him; it seemed that to Creed, what you had to say was more important than what he had to say. And when you think about it, it makes sense that a record producer *should* have that kind of attitude and approach. If you listen to what the musician has to say, he'll feel more a part of the process, and his creativity will flower. If you listen to what your bosses have to say—and take their suggestions to heart—they'll learn to trust you, and thus be more apt to let you either do exactly what you want or experiment with something new. And if you listen to what record buyers have to say, you'll make records they'll hopefully buy.

Among jazz folks, Creed had a reputation for doing what needed to be done to sell records—and sometimes doing what needed to be done meant including a Beatles cover on his artist's album, which some people thought was a no-no—but a lot of these folks didn't realize that Creed got his start at Bethlehem Records, where he worked with distinctly noncommercial artists like bassists Charles Mingus and Oscar Pettiford, and trumpeter Ruby Braff. And then, in 1960, he founded Impulse Records, and man, what a label that was: John

Coltrane, Duke Ellington, Gil Evans, Oliver Nelson, and on and on and on. In 1961, I guess Verve made Creed an offer he couldn't refuse, so he left Impulse, and next thing you know, he's turning Stan Getz into a bossa nova star.

I'm sure that Creed Taylor looked at Wes Montgomery in the same way he looked at Stan Getz: a cat that could play both accessibly and substantially, a flexible musician who could thrive in any setting, and with any material. Wes's first record with Verve and Creed, *Movin' Wes*, was unlike anything Wes had ever done, and man, I dug it. Creed put Wes in front of a big band—up to that point, few, if any, guitarists were ever featured as a soloist in front of a big band—and had him play a nice blend of standards, originals, and pop tunes. The formula worked; it became Wes's best-selling record to date.

I loved how the folks at Verve handled Wes's career—they mixed it up, and let him tear it up with small groups and big bands. One record, you'd hear him wailing away with Miles Davis's rhythm section of Wynton Kelly, Paul Chambers, and Jimmy Cobb, and the next, he'd be back in front of a big band, cutting classics like "Bumpin'" and "Goin' Out of My Head." He kept his old fans, brought in new fans, and reached a level of popularity worthy of his talents.

But here's the tough part: Creed and his right-hand man Esmond Edwards saw me as the next Wes Montgomery, and that was at once flattering and blasphemous. See, nobody was as good as Wes, nobody was as elegant or as technically proficient. And I'd developed my own thing; I had some quirks and some tricks, and if you listened carefully to what I was doing, you might say, "Hey, I've heard that sound before. Who is that cat? He sounds familiar." Over time, I found my voice, and while I suppose there might've been a small bit of Wes in there, I didn't want to be the next Wes Montgomery. I wanted to be the first George Benson. Besides, there was only one Wes Montgomery, and there would never be another.

My first record for Verve was called *Giblet Gravy*, and I'd never done anything like it—the closest I'd come was back in 1964, with

The Brother Jack McDuff Quartet with the Big Band of Benny Golson. But this time, it was up to me to carry the session, to ride the wave of a large ensemble, and unlike that 1964 session, I wasn't scared. As a matter of fact, I had a blast.

Esmond hired a cat named Tom McIntosh to do the arrangements, and those arrangements were terrific, smart and swinging, with something for everybody to enjoy. During a break, Tom said to me, "Man, you look familiar. I know I've seen you before."

"Did you see me play with Jack McDuff?"

"No."

"Did you spend any time in Pittsburgh in the late 1950s?"

"No." Then he snapped. "You know what? You look just like this guy I was in the army with. Carlos was his name. Close, close friend."

I shrugged. "Sorry. I don't know anybody named Carlos."

"Carlos wasn't his real name," Tom said. "That's just what we called him. His real name was Charles. Charles Evans."

"*Whaaaaaaaat?* That's my father!" And that was the beginning of a lifelong friendship.

The band on *Giblet Gravy*, well, those were some of the heaviest cats I'd ever played with. You've got Herbie Hancock, who, thanks to all those records he recorded with Miles—*ESP, Miles Smiles, The Sorcerer*—was the hottest piano player in the world. You've got Ron Carter and Bob Cranshaw switching off on the bass, and that was a special thing for a guy who'd spent the majority of his professional life playing in bands that got the bass notes from an organ. You've got Billy Cobham, a little twenty-three-year-old who, only a few years later, would be considered one of jazz's finest drummers. (Before the session, I told Ron that Elvin Jones—John Coltrane's genius percussionist—was my favorite drummer, but Ron said, "Billy's better." That got my attention.) And you've got a big band and background vocalists who were so good they made me feel like I was Charlie Parker cutting his records for Norman Granz's company. Not that I sounded like Charlie Parker—I wasn't even close—but what with all these talented folks working with me, I could pretend. Sometimes, I didn't pretend well enough.

I was working on one of the tunes—it might've been that standard ballad "What's New"—and I was reading the chart (not well), playing all these wrong chord changes—*brrrrp . . . braappppp . . . bzzzzz*—concerned that I'd never get it under my fingers. From the corner of the room, a figure emerged, a young cat who ran over, picked up my music, and said, "George, let me see that." Then he held out his hands and said, "Let me borrow that."

I thought, *Who's this cat? Where's he from? I'm on Verve, and he's just hanging out. I'm Billy the Kid, man—who does he think he is, trying to come into my town and take over?* After he donned my axe, he said, "Here's what these chords sound like." And then, *brrrrrrrring . . . brrrrrring . . . brrrrrrrrrrrring*, there they were, the right chords, played beautifully and perfectly. And then he began to play some licks and chords of his own. His guitar playing was so unusual; he had his own niche. He read music fluently, had a great sound, great rhythm, and he was just . . . great. I thought, *Dang, I better leave this cat alone.*

I said, "Hey, man, thanks! What's your name?"

"Eric Gale."

Later on that day, after Eric had split, I asked around about him, and more than one person said, "Eric Gale is *baaaaad*. He's hot. You're almost as good as he is. *Almost.*"

I thought, *Man, if I'm even almost as good as he is, I'm doing okay.* I decided it was a bad idea to turn music into a competition—I've felt that way ever since—and, as was the case with Tom McIntosh, Eric and I became friends for life.

The next day, I sat down with Esmond to discuss the material we were going to do with Herbie and Ron. Remember, those two were the best of the best, so I knew I had to do everything in my power to keep up, and to make sure that what we came up with was worthy of their talents. So I asked Esmond, "Can we get a conga player?"

He was silent and expressionless, so I had no idea whether he thought auxiliary percussion made sense. Finally, he asked, "Why?"

I said, "Sometimes the rhythm gets away on me. Sometimes I don't know where I'm at." That was a hard admission, but Esmond was a good man, and I thought he'd appreciate my honesty, especially since it was in the best interest of the record. "If we have some congas back there, I think things'll even out for me." What I didn't say was, *I don't want to look bad in front of Herbie and Ron.*

Esmond nodded. "I bet I could get Johnny Pacheco. I'm pretty sure he's in town. You'll dig him. Nice cat. And he's recorded with Kenny Burrell and McCoy Tyner."

My smile probably blinded him. "Man, if he worked with Kenny and McCoy, he can darn sure work with me!" Sure enough, Johnny was available, and when he arrived at the studio a couple hours later, he, Herbie, Ron, and I went to work on a rendition of Charlie Parker's classic 12-bar blues, "Billie's Bounce."

If you'll permit me another one of my digressions, I'd like to discuss "trading fours." In the early days of bebop, Charlie Parker and Dizzy Gillespie set the template for jazz small-band arrangements. The lead instruments played the "head"—that's what jazz cats call the main melodies—then the lead instruments—in their case, it was Bird's sax and Diz's trumpet—took a few solo choruses, followed by piano, then sometimes bass. The next logical soloist would be the drummer, but sometimes an unaccompanied drum solo kills a tune's momentum, so somebody came up with the concept of "trading fours," which is more or less exactly what it sounds like: One cat improvises for four bars, then the drummer follows suit. Then another cat, then the drummer, then the first cat, then the drummer again, and so on, until it's time to go back to the head. Eventually, folks decided that trading fours shouldn't be limited to going back and forth with the drummer. Sometimes the entire band traded fours with one another, sometimes the bass and piano traded fours, and sometimes the two horn players traded fours. It was a great way to demonstrate band communication, because when it's done correctly—when the musicians are really listening to one another—it sounds seamless, like one soloist playing different instruments.

Now I dug trading fours, so after we ran through the tune a couple of times, I suggested Herbie and I do so before the final time through the head. Herbie was an affable sort, so he agreed. Thing is, he was better at it than me. *Way* better. He had the uncanny knack of being able to pick up exactly where I left off, then taking it to another level and turning it into something special. Then, when it came back to me, things went back to normal. When I suggested fours, I was too dumb to realize that I was messing with a boss, and after about two choruses of going around, him and me, me and him, I thought, *I'd better get out of this while I'm still alive here*, so I played the head, and I survived my trading fours with Herbie more or less unscathed.

But I must've done something right, because a few days later the phone rang, and there was this raspy voice on the other end of the line, a voice that was known to every jazz musician and jazz fan across the world, a voice belonging to one Miles Dewey Davis III. And I freaked out.

See, in 1967, Miles was at the top of the jazz list, a true star. He'd carved out a niche for himself that was more unique than any other in music history. He didn't play loud, fast trumpet like Pops or Diz, but he created a sound and an approach that was completely his own, and nobody else could replicate it. His tone was magnificent—punchy, full, and weighty, with no vibrato—and it was all his own. If you wanted somebody on your record who sounded like Miles Davis, you had to hire Miles Davis, period.

In what I soon found out was typical Miles fashion, he got right down to business: "I want to make a record. With you." There was a small part of me that wondered if it was one of my friends playing a trick on me. But after we spoke for a few more minutes, I knew it was him, because he spoke in this gravelly voice that everybody impersonated but nobody got *right*. His voice was so froggy that I could barely understand all of what he was saying, but he managed to get one thing across, loud and clear: *I want you to come to a recording session of mine tomorrow.*

After I hung up, I stared at the wall for a good long while, the same question blowing through my head over and over again: *What am I gonna play on a Miles Davis record?* I didn't come up with a good answer—for that matter, I didn't come up with *any* answer— but I went to the studio anyhow. Even if it was a disaster, at least I'd get to play with Herbie and Ron again.

When I arrived at Columbia Studio B, Herbie and Ron were set up and ready to go, as were Miles's saxophonist, Wayne Shorter, and his drummer, Tony Williams. Teo Macero, the producer, dialed in the levels; then we were ready to roll. Miles wandered in about an hour later. Then, without saying a word, he took his trumpet from his case, jammed in the mouthpiece, leaned into his microphone, and *brrrrrrrp*, played a single note. As we all waited for some instruction, he removed the mouthpiece, packed up his instrument, and walked out.

And that was it.

Nobody seemed particularly surprised, but I wasn't surprised that nobody was surprised—after all, Miles had been known to cancel concerts at the last minute, concerts for which he was being paid $20,000, and if he was willing to pull the plug on that kind of money, he'd certainly be willing to pull the plug on a midweek studio session with a semi-obscure guitarist named George Benson. After Miles had left the building, Teo told us, "Okay, gentleman, you know the drill. Let's try it again tomorrow."

Next day, Miles did the exact same thing: Walked in, removed the trumpet, inserted the mouthpiece, *brrrrrrrp*, then packed up. On his way out, Teo said, "Miles, what's the problem? What can we do for you?" From the exhausted, exasperated tone of his voice, it sounded as though he'd had this conversation with Miles *many* times before.

"First of all, this microphone sounds like a tin can," Miles growled.

He said, "We can fix that. What else do you need?"

Miles's answer was to turn around and split. After a few moments of awkward silence, I said, "Well, I guess he ain't coming back." Nobody responded, so we all packed up and went home. I resolved not to return if I was asked. It was too humiliating.

The next day, sure enough, Miles called. "You coming into the studio tomorrow?" he rasped.

I said, "Miles, man, why should I show up? You ain't gonna play anything. And I don't want to take your money if I'm not gonna do nothing."

He said, "Just be there. I'll make some music. Don't worry about it."

"Okay. See you tomorrow." So much for my strong resolution.

The next day, before Miles even took off his jacket, Teo asked him, "Why'd you take off outta here the last couple of days, man? The real reason."

Miles glared at the producer, then said, "Man, when I asked you for a guitar player, why'd you send Joe Beck?" Joe Beck was an excellent young session guitarist who was making a name for himself as a jazz/rock player. "You know *they* can't swing."

The studio got *real* quiet *real* fast, because everybody knew what Miles meant by "they"—white guys. I looked over at Teo and a welcome visitor by the name of John Hammond—both of whom were white—and was so embarrassed for them that I wanted to crawl under a table.

Teo, however, didn't look the least bit fazed. He said, "We know what we're doing, Miles. Trust us. Let's just play some music."

The two stared silently at each other for a bit, then Miles shook his head and finally went about the business of recording. We tried a few ideas, some of which worked and some of which didn't, then, during a break, Tony Williams came over and, in his high little voice, said, "George, you know, when you get to that next section, you should try to . . ."

Before he could finish the sentence, Miles growled, "Man, shut up, Tony! Go back there and play your drums! Don't tell nobody else how to play!" He then pointed to the back of the studio and said, "Furthermore, set your drums up by the wall. You're too loud!"

For the rest of the day, Tony barely said a word.

After the break, we started rehearsing the craziest song I ever heard in my life, a Wayne Shorter tune that made no sense to me. (Wayne was one of the greatest small-band composers in jazz history, but a lot of his tunes didn't make sense upon first listening. But after you listened to them several times, they started to sound beautiful, and you wondered why you were confused in the first place.) Miles said, "Wayne, what kind of song is this? I think you write these crazy tunes just to hang me up, just to see if I can play them."

Frankly, I felt the same way.

We rehearsed for an hour or so, never once looking at Wayne's chart, because I knew it wouldn't do me any good. Miles wasn't one for specific instruction, so once we finally got rolling on the tune, I was on my own. I just listened to what they were doing and tried to find something to play, some way to get into this tune. But after a while, I finally found a groove, and I stuck with it, because I'd learned that once I found a spot that was comfortable, I should stay there. (Folks seemed to like that, which I suppose was why I kept getting hired by heavies like saxophonists Lou Donaldson and Hank Mobley, and organists Larry Young and Jimmy Smith.) Eventually I played a few hot licks here and there, even though I didn't even really know what key we were in. I looked at Miles, and he seemed pleased—I think he liked it when I rambled and rumbled, when I tried something that was outside of my comfort zone. And to tell the truth, most of what happened that afternoon and evening was *well* out of my comfort zone.

The funny part about the whole thing is that from the day that album, *Miles in the Sky*, was released, folks would come up to me and say, "Man, I like what you did on that Miles Davis record."

To which I'd always reply, "Man, I was just noodling! I didn't *do* anything!"

There's a postscript to all this, of which I am not proud.

A few months later, an ugly thought crept into my head: *Maybe what Miles was saying at that session was right. This is our music, black people's music.* I went down that trail for a bit, until I ran into my fellow Pittsburgh native Art Blakey. Art was one of the few old-school beboppers still playing bebop, and he'd been there and done that several times over, so when he spoke, you listened.

I launched into my theories about who owns jazz, and after about three sentences, Art held up his hand and said, "George, let me tell you something, man: Jazz music has been nurtured by all kinds of people—including white people. White folks' contribution to jazz is invaluable. Jazz music is *not* only black people's music. At the beginning, yeah, it was, but not now. The reason the music is where it is today is because blacks and whites have worked together to advance it."

I just gawked at Art, then said, "Wowwwww." That was all I *could* say: "Wowwwww." Because it only takes a few words from somebody in whom you truly believe to change *everything*. And I can state unequivocally that there are great jazz musicians of all races, creeds, colors, genders, and ages. There're great Mexican musicians, Cuban musicians, Puerto Rican musicians, European musicians—everywhere in the world, there're cats who can play their tails off. And I can vouch for that, because I played with them.

A few months later, word got back to me that Miles was going to ask me to join his band. (I don't recall who delivered the news. Might've been Herbie. Might've been Ron. The thought that Miles Davis would consider hiring George Benson was so mind-blowing that the moment was a blur.) Miles was good to me at the session, and I knew he wasn't good to just anybody, so I thought, *Oh man, I'm in like Flynn. I'm gonna be playing all over the world for captive audiences, I'm gonna get paid a regular salary—and hopefully a good one—I'm gonna be flying first-class and staying at four-star hotels and, best of all, I'll be sharing the bandstand with Miles, Wayne, Herbie, Ron, and Tony. I'll become a true musician!*

I called Jimmy Boyd with the news. He said, without hesitation, "You can't do it."

My chin hit my chest. "What do you mean, I can't do it? This is the opportunity of a lifetime!"

"Everybody at the record company says you're going to be bigger than Miles," Jimmy explained.

I said, "Say what? Bigger than Miles?" That was absurd. Miles played with Charlie Parker, Miles invented cool, Miles resurrected hard bop, Miles practically created jazz fusion. Me, I cut a few records on my own and almost got switchbladed by my former bandleader. "Who is that you've been talking to at the record company?"

He ducked the question. "Yeah, man, that's what they're saying. They're saying they think you're going to be bigger than Miles."

I said, "I wonder why they're thinking that?"

"I don't know, man, but I like it."

When I hung up with Jimmy, I started thinking about my place in the jazz world. To an extent, I'd been living in a vacuum, focusing all of my energy on gigging and recording, not paying attention to what the outside world had to say about me or how my playing stacked up against the other guitarists on the scene.

But other folks were paying attention, and most had formed an opinion of what I was and what I could be. The Verve team seemed to have a little respect for my potential—certainly more so than the Columbia team had—but I didn't consider those sorts of things because I just wanted to play some guitar, to make some good records, to perform some good shows, and, most importantly, to *hustle*. I knew for certain that the hustling was paying off: My band was working forty-eight weeks a year. My hard work was also paying off—my chops were better than they'd ever been—but I didn't realize how much my technique had improved until cats started mentioning it and comparing me to people like John McLaughlin.

John had just come over from England, and word on the street was that he was the fastest guitar player in the world. And not only did he have chops, but he used them wisely. John didn't play fast simply for the sake of playing fast; his ideas flowed so hard that utilizing speed was the only way he could get them out.

The first time I met John was at a club in Harlem in 1969, with the Tony Williams Lifetime. The Lifetime was an organ trio featuring John, Tony, and my old friend Larry Young, but they had nothing to do with the organ trios of my youth. They were loud, man, loud and out there—a mixture of jazz, rock, avant-garde, and noise. Were they a good band? Heck, yeah. Would I have been able to play their sort of music? Heck, no.

When I stopped by their rehearsal to say hello and meet John, Tony ran over and asked, "George, can we borrow your amp?" He knew I had a big old great-sounding Fender that would fill up the club beautifully.

I wondered why they needed an amplifier at the last minute like that. Did the promoter not provide one? Was John's in a back room somewhere at LaGuardia Airport? Did the same Harlem thugs who used to steal my hubcaps in front of Minton's sneak into the club and rip it off? Tony was a good cat, so I didn't press him. "Yeah, you all can borrow my amp. Go ahead, use it. Have fun."

I picked it up the following afternoon, then took it straight to the club where I was gigging that night. After I set up, I noticed that all the dials on my Fender were jacked up to ten: the volume, the bass, the midrange, the treble, the master volume, *everything*. I said aloud, "What in the world is this?" then turned the knobs down to a rational level, plugged in, and strummed. Nothing. I jiggled the chord and fiddled the knobs. Still nothing. Turned out that John McLaughlin had blown out my amplifier.

Eventually I saw John play, and man, he deserved the accolades, as well as his place in Miles Davis's band. He was so different from everybody else out there: his nonlinear approach, his embracing of rock and world-music sounds, and, of course, his ridiculous technique. Soon, a promoter hooked us up for a gig at Lincoln Center in New York; I'm sure he was hoping for a guitar gunfight at the O.K. Corral. When we walked out onstage, John sat down on a stool—I always played standing up at live shows—and he set his equalizer so it sounded like he was playing a sitar. I didn't know what to do with that, so I just did my thing and let him do his.

After the gig, I asked him, "John, why did you try and do a sitar thing?"

"I did it to avoid you, George," he said in his charming English accent. "I didn't want any of that contest stuff. I don't want people comparing us, so I did something completely different."

I said, "You know what? I was thinking the same thing. I just didn't know how to go about it."

He smiled. "The whole time, I was thinking, 'Man, I'm gonna get killed in here.'"

"I was thinking the exact same thing!" I said. That was the first night of a lifelong friendship.

On June 15, 1968, Wes Montgomery passed away at the young, young age of forty-five, and man, that was a blow like you wouldn't believe. He was such an inspirational figure, both as a musician and a man. I wish more people had looked to Wes as a role model, because he was the consummate professional. He always made his gigs, always gave his all, always practiced every day, always treated his sidemen with the respect they deserved, and always played his backside off. Wes Montgomery left me some incredible things to think about, both musically and extra-musically, and he left the world a legacy of experiments that were his own, and almost always without fail, his experimentation worked beautifully. By examining those experiments and by watching him interact with the world at large, I *understood*. You don't find too many people like that in the arts. Heck, you don't find too many people like that in *life*.

Though I had plenty of love for the other guitar players of my generation, none of them inspired me like Wes. Right after he passed, one of the TV networks reran a 1967 special starring Herb Alpert, a trumpet player who was the "A" half of A&M Records. Wes was one of the guests, and when Herb introduced him, he said, with great flourish, "Ladies and gentlemen, my favorite guitar player, Wes Montgomery." Herb then sat down on a stool next to Wes and gave him a long, warm hug. I thought, *Man, that's impressive. Wes is finally a real star.* After Wes played a phenomenal version of "Goin' Out of My Head," I said aloud, "Someday, I want that to be me."

What I didn't know was that right around the time of the original airing—possibly even that night—Wes said to Herb Alpert, "You ever heard of a kid named George Benson?"

Herb said, "No."

"You will," Wes said, and that's *all* he said. "You will." See, Wes wasn't the type of guy to force somebody to do something he didn't want to do; he wouldn't tell Herb, "Sign this cat," and possibly put Herb in the awkward position of saying no to a pal and business associate. Wes would want Herb to make his own decision without feeling pressured. He could've parlayed his power and friendship into a deal for me but knew that it would be better in the long run if I got an offer based on my own merit.

At this point, my old friend Creed Taylor was working at A&M. Herb knew that Creed always had his ear to the ground, so Herb asked Creed, "Do you know a kid named George Benson?"

Creed said, "As a matter of fact I do." (I wonder if Creed was surprised that a guy like Herb didn't know who I was. I wasn't a star by any means, but at that point, I'd been on the jazz scene for almost ten years.)

"Wes told me he's *baaaaad*. You think you could get him for our label?" Herb asked.

"I'll try."

Sometime thereafter, I was in the kitchen at the Village Vanguard, getting ready to take the stage, and who should poke his head in but Creed Taylor. As usual, he didn't say much—remember, Creed was a quiet cat—but we exchanged pleasantries, and even though he only uttered a few words, I somehow sensed he had something brewing. Sure enough, he hooked us up with A&M Records, for whom I cut three albums.

The first one was called *Shape of Things to Come*, which featured a photo of me on the back cover, half naked. (I can say with authority that that was *not* the shape of things to come.) Creed was in charge, and I had very little say in any aspect of the record, from the material, to the musicians, to the half-naked picture of me. There were things that went on with which I wasn't particularly pleased, but I was so happy to be in an environment where people knew what they were doing that I kept my mouth shut. (I'm not saying that to disparage Columbia or Verve, mind you. It's just that Herb Alpert was a musician, and he knew what musicians needed from their label.) I didn't want to make waves, because we all shared one goal: to find an audience. The following year, we cut *The Other Side of Abbey Road*, on which we covered most of the Beatles' final album, and man, critics all over the world hated that one.

(Fortunately for me, Paul McCartney either dug the album or didn't hear it, and I say that because if he had issues with the record, he might not have wanted to have anything to do with me. As it turned out, we met several years later and became solid pals. In 2006 I was cutting an album with vocalist Al Jarreau—one of the most beautiful cats you'll ever meet—called *Givin' It Up*. Al and I were laying down the Sam Cooke tune "Bring It on Home to Me," and in walks Paul, who came by partly to see me but mostly to meet Al. As we listened to the playback, I asked Paul, "Do you know this song, man?"

He said, "Yeah, I know it." Of course he did. Paul McCartney is a walking rock 'n' soul encyclopedia and knows *every* song.

"You wanna get a piece of this?"

He thought about it long and hard, then said, "Not right now, because I'm next door doing my own thing. But I'll come back when I'm done."

Now Paul is one of the kindest men in the music industry, so there was a chance he was saying that just to be nice. But after he left, I thought, *You know something? He just might come back and do that.* And sure enough, the next day, he burst into the studio and said, "Cue up that bloody Cooke song. I'll try a take." Actually, he tried two or three takes, and man, that Beatle *killed* it.)

As much as I loved working with Herb, it was clear that the label and I weren't a good match, so our stay over at A&M ended almost as quickly as it began.

A few weeks later, I got a phone call: Creed. "George, I'm starting my own label. Do you want to be . . ."

Before he could even finish the question, I said, "Yes, I very much want to be on it. What's it gonna be called?"

"Creed Taylor Incorporated."

"That's a mouthful," I said.

"Yeah. It is. So we're going by CTI Records. Does that sound better?"

"Man, that sounds great!"

Interlude #3

Miles Ahead and Miles Beyond

Though we never again shared the recording studio, Miles Davis and I maintained a relationship, both personally and professionally. The personal part was a periodic late-night phone call in which he'd rasp a question, an opinion, or a random tidbit, then go on his way, disappearing into the ozone for who knows how long. (There was a reason his nickname was the Prince of Darkness.) The professional part was our bands sharing concert bills.

Throughout his career, Miles had played hundreds of jazz festivals and dozens of rock fests, so he knew what it was like to be one band among twenty. But when it came to his own gigs, he was used to being the Man. It was his show and his band, and the crowd knew if they wanted to see Miles, they'd darn well better show up on time, because he rarely, if ever, had an opening band.

When things started picking up for me—when my band developed a following of its own—Miles and I did some gigs together. The majority of the time, he was the headliner, but once in a while, I'd top the bill, and, man, that sometimes got ugly. See, much of the audience assumed that Miles would close the show, so when they showed up late, and I was onstage doing my thing, there was some anger. Once word got back to Miles and his people that there were some unhappy customers, he never let us headline again. And that didn't upset or insult me in the least. Miles was the number one star, and even though he passed away in 1991, he always will be.

But there was a minute or two when I didn't feel that way, a minute or two when I believed I was so hot that during these Davis/ Benson gigs I had the right to play longer than my allotted time. I quickly learned that was a terrible idea. The second time that happened, Miles cussed me out so badly that my ears are still ringing.

See, Miles was still the star, the person who everyone wanted to see, the mystic, the unpredictable legend. And I understood that because I dug his unpredictability—you never knew what the cat was going to do next, and you always wanted to know, because no matter what, it would be interesting. Maybe it would be a scary record or a freaky interview or an insane concert, but if you missed it, you were missing something, because Miles Davis is, was, and always will be jazz's greatest mover and shaker, the slickest cat in the world.

7 The Sound of the Seventies

Most folks think that Creed Taylor Incorporated launched in 1970, but the fact is, CTI had been in existence for three years . . . sort of. And I say "sort of," because many of the records Creed produced for A&M had a tiny little CTI logo somewhere on the cover. Despite all the good work Creed had done at A&M—and Verve and Bethlehem and Impulse—he wasn't very liquid, so when it came time to launch the label, he had to borrow a whole lot of money. That didn't scare me off; see, I had faith in Creed, plus I was as confident in my playing as I'd ever been, because I'd been working, and working hard, keeping up my forty-eight-weeks-a-year gigging schedule. My chops were in great shape, my band was tight, and I was *ready*.

Creed didn't have enough money to bring in his usual string section or big band—heck, he didn't have enough bread to hire an arranger, let alone fifteen more musicians—so I had to figure out a way to make the record special. Since I felt so good about what I was doing on the guitar, I thought, *I'll just get some great cats, pick some great tunes, and play some great guitar.* And that's exactly what I did.

I borrowed Miles Davis's drummer—Jack DeJohnette—and brought Ron Carter aboard, so I thought it would be appropriate to honor Miles with a funky cover of "So What," his classic modal tune from *Kind of Blue.* We also experimented with some Middle Eastern vibes, some bossa nova, and some good old bebop. Why the diversity?

Well, we just wanted to show what we could do, as if to say, *If you don't like this, try that, and if you don't like that, try this.* I hadn't cut what could be called a straight-ahead jazz album since 1966, which was probably why people seemed (happily) surprised with the result.

Some of Creed's albums started to make some noise—one of which was Stanley Turrentine's *Sugar*, a record on which, as previously noted, I'm proud to have played; and man, Freddie Hubbard sounded great on that one—and the upstart label head got a few dollars together, so he was able to keep a stable of the baddest cats of the day, agreeable cats like Stanley, Freddie, Herbie, Ron, Jack DeJohnette, Billy Cobham, flute genius Hubert Laws, saxophone heavy Joe Farrell . . . I could go on. It was a family, similar to what went on at Prestige in the 1950s—pianist Mal Waldron, bassist Doug Watkins, and drummer Art Taylor turned up on a whole lot of the label's records—and Blue Note in the 1960s—there, you were looking at a bunch of Hank Mobley's tenor, Lee Morgan's trumpet, and McCoy Tyner's piano. CTI was a good place to be.

Freddie's *First Light* was one of my first CTI sessions, at once slick and rich—full of interesting tunes, hip arrangements by Creed's favorite arranger Don Sebesky, and some killer playing from Mr. Hubbard. This was 1971, when Freddie was at the height of his considerable powers, and since Miles Davis had gone in a direction that was a bit confusing to fans of his "My Funny Valentine"–era work, *First Light* helped Freddie become *Downbeat* magazine's number one trumpeter, edging out Miles by a hair. Freddie and I were friends, but after that, he *really* loved me, because he thought I helped him climb to the top of the list.

He'd call me up and say, "George, I'm the number one trumpet player in the world, man, *the number one trumpeter in the world!*"

I'd laugh, then say, "Don't be braggin' on it, man. Just let it ride." But I couldn't get on Freddie too much because he wasn't really bragging—he was excited, like a little kid. After all, this was something he probably never thought could happen, and if all of his friends, family, fellow musicians, and fans were applauding him, who was I to rain on his parade?

Even though Freddie and I weren't competitive people, we were thrown into a competition at the 1972 Grammy Awards, when *First Light* was nominated alongside my album *White Rabbit*. (The other nominees were Joe Farrell's *Outback*—another CTI record—Weather Report's *I Sing the Body Electric*, and Chuck Mangione's *The Chuck Mangione Quartet*. That's some serious company, man, and I was thrilled to even be considered. Whether it's for a Grammy, an Oscar, or an Emmy, you'll hear cats say, "It's an honor just to be nominated." It's become a cliché, but I can tell you with complete honesty that it's 100 percent true. And believe me, it never gets old. Whenever I get that call, I feel like I did back in '72, back when I was practically a baby.) When *First Light* won, I was nothing but happy for Freddie, and I told him, "Hey, man, nobody ever nominated me for anything. And I played on your Grammy-winning record! *Right on*."

Whenever I gigged with Freddie I *learned*, be it something about phrasing, a new way to outline a chord, or how to build a solo. But apparently it was reciprocal: "George," he once told me, "I went out and got a transcription of one of your solos, and I couldn't even play the damn thing, not even close. That's some weird stuff you're doing on there."

I said, "Man, I don't even think about it. I just play it."

Freddie just shook his head and chuckled.

Coincidentally, Miles rang me up not too long thereafter. (It was always an event when Miles called; it was like a phone call from the right-brain side of outer space. You knew that whatever you discussed—music, boxing, cars, whatever—the conversation would be memorable.) After I said hello, he said, without preamble, "What do you think about when you play, George?"

"Oh, man, get out of here!" I laughed, because I thought he was kidding around. I mean, Miles Davis asking George Benson what he thought about when he played? *Crazy.* "I should be asking *you* what it is *you* do."

"No, I'm serious. I want to know what it is you think about when you play."

"Come on, man. Stop messing with me."

"I'm not messing with you, George. I really want to know. What is it you're thinking?" (Folks who know anything about Miles Davis's, shall we say, colorful vocabulary won't be surprised to learn that there were a few curse words sprinkled in there.)

We went back and forth like that for about ten more minutes, until, after trying and failing to explain my thought process, I said, "Man, I don't know what the heck I'm thinking about when I play. I just bounce from one thing to another."

After a beat, Miles said, "That's it?"

"Okay, after I left McDuff, I used to practice *so much*, and I developed a theory that when you practice all the time, you *really* remember ten percent of whatever it is you're working on; the other ninety percent is about chops maintenance. So if you practice a hundred things, you'll absorb ten of them, and if you practice a thousand things, you'll absorb one hundred, and if you practice ten thousand things, you'll have a thousand. I figured the more I absorbed, the less chance there was that I'd run out of ideas, and if I had a lot of licks in my bloodstream, I could just bounce from one thing to another, and it'd sound okay. And I think it works. Sometimes, I'll be on a long gig, like six hours over six sets, and I'll never run out of licks."

Miles was quiet for bit, then said, "Thanks, man," and hung up.

A few minutes later, it dawned on me that I didn't mention that my thought process was shaped in part by what kind of music I listened to. I always went back to my organ records: Jimmy Smith, Johnny "Hammond" Smith, Jimmy McGriff, and Groove Holmes—heck, every once in a while, I even pulled out something by Brother Jack

McDuff—but I listened to more than records featuring guitarists. I checked out Charlie Parker's stuff on Savoy, and Art Tatum's stuff on Capitol, and even Miles's stuff on Prestige. I listened to everything, and even if I didn't dig what was going on, I knew that if I paid close attention I could still pick up *something*.

Even though it didn't take home the Grammy, *White Rabbit* was a big record for us for a few reasons. First off, there was the excellent playing courtesy of Mr. Hancock and Mr. Cobham, the hip arrangements courtesy of Mr. Sebesky, and the interesting tune selection courtesy of Mr. Taylor. But there was another factor that may have played into its success: Creed didn't put my photo on the cover.

Now I'm not a vain guy, not the sort of person who has to have my face plastered on album jackets and promotional posters in order to satisfy my ego. My first instinct is to go with whatever looks the coolest, and if it's a shot of me playing a guitar—which was the case on *Bad Benson*, my CTI record from 1973—great. If it's a picture of a red wall with a white-rimmed window—which was the case on *Body Talk*, my CTI record from 1974—that's great, too. But the cover of *White Rabbit*, combined with the rock/pop-oriented material (i.e., the Jefferson Airplane title cut, and "California Dreamin'" by the Mamas and the Papas) sometimes played on a mellow acoustic guitar, gave people a mistaken impression about me.

To wit: Soon after the record hit the streets, I was at my local guitar store, picking up some strings and picks. There were two cats in line behind me, discussing what they were going to do that night. "Who's at the club?" one asked.

"Some guy named George Benson."

"Never heard of him. Who is it?"

"He's a guitar player. A white guy. He plays like Howard Roberts."

I thought, *What? A white guy? Howard Roberts?*

Now bear in mind that Howard Roberts was an excellent guitarist. Howard had been on and off the scene since the mid-1950s, but in the early 1970s, he cut a couple of nice records for Impulse that had garnered him some notoriety. But from my perspective, we didn't sound at all alike, and I think if those guys had seen my black self on the cover of *White Rabbit*, they wouldn't have thought to compare me to a white guitarist. Which begs the question, would they have been any more or any less interested in coming to my show or buying the record if they knew I was black? Which begs yet another question: Was this something Creed considered when he was figuring out what the cover should look like? But then I remembered what Art Blakey had told me about jazz and race, and I decided to let it go, to let my music speak for itself. If somebody didn't buy my records or go to my shows because they didn't like whatever color they thought I was, I figured it was their loss.

About those shows: In terms of audience numbers, they used to be so-so, but once all the CTI albums started popping, there were lines around the corner at virtually all of my gigs. We were moving up in the world, even though we didn't have a big record. Now, we had some *good* records but not a *big* one, and there's a difference—and that difference manifests itself in what size venue you've booked. Nobody was hiring us to play auditoriums and concert halls. We were still in the clubs, but they were good clubs, not dives—sophisticated clubs with sophisticated audiences. And those sophisticated audiences were seeing what I thought was a pretty good band, even though it might not have been what they were expecting. See, the jazz world was changing. The organ was going out, and the electric piano was coming in . . . and that's something that was initially tough on a guy like Ronnie Foster.

I met Ronnie, a native of Buffalo, New York, when he was fifteen, and the second I heard him play, I knew the kid was a genius, and I honestly believed that if he worked hard and stayed on a good path, he'd end up being one of the greatest jazz musicians of all time. See, Ronnie was a free thinker. He didn't sit down at the piano with an encyclopedia of licks at his disposal—he was a true improviser who made up everything as he went along, *everything*, and it was always something different, *always*. You didn't know where he was going to end up—I don't think he knew, either—but wherever and whenever he landed, your socks were knocked off. Even though he was still a child, I wanted him to join my band. The opportunity to watch a young cat with that much innate talent grow and evolve would've been a treat.

Naturally, he wanted to go with me—what teenager wouldn't?—but he had to get his parents' approval, so he brought me to his house to meet his folks. Before I could even get two words out, his mother tugged on my sleeve and begged, "Mr. Benson, please don't take my son out of here. I want him to finish high school."

Without a moment's hesitation, I said, "Okay, Mrs. Foster, I will not take him out on the road." See, it's never a good idea to disrespect a mother's wish. Ronnie was devastated, but he kept on playing his organ, kept on being a genius. When he graduated from high school a couple years later, he gave his mother his diploma, and then he left to go out on the road that same night. But not with me.

I ran into him a few years later, and he was still playing some mean organ . . . but he wasn't happy about it. Aside from the fact that he was having some domestic problems, he was tired of his instrument and the life of a musician. "George," he told me, "I don't want to play organ no more. I don't never want to play nothing, as long as I live."

Feeling like a parent trying to point his kid down the straight and narrow, I put my hand on his shoulder and said, "That'll change, Ronnie. You're fighting with a girl, you're young, and you haven't had enough life experiences to offer you perspective. Right now, everything feels like it's life and death. Trust me, that'll change."

He shrugged. "Yeah, maybe."

"But listen, if you want to take some time away to get your head together and you need someplace to put your organ, you can put it in the studio in my garage."

After a few weeks of watching over Ronnie's Hammond B-3, I gave him a call: "Hey, man, I need an organ player, and all the other guys out there are spoken for." That wasn't really true. I didn't call "all the other guys." I called Ronnie.

He hemmed and hawed for a few minutes, then finally said, "Okay, George, I'll do it. But I'm only doing it for you." So he did it, and he fit with us, hand in glove. Unfortunately for him, that was right when organs were going the way of the Model T. It was all about electric keyboards, synthesizers, and Fender Rhodes.

What that meant for me was that I had to retool. Since organs were out of vogue, I had to find not only an electric pianist but also a bassist. (If you'll recall, bassists weren't necessary when there was a B-3 in the band, because the organist played the bass notes.) The first thing I did was ask Ronnie if he'd be willing to switch instruments.

He made a nasty face, like he'd eaten five lemons. "Man, I'm not no piano player. I play organ, not piano, and I don't think . . ."

"Ronnie, listen, listen, listen. I know that, for sure. I know you're not a pianist, but I need a Fender Rhodes player. That's almost like an organ." It took me half an hour to convince him to come up to Canada with us and give it a shot. After his first solo during the first song on the first set, the place went berserk, and he got the biggest round of applause he'd ever gotten in his life. It went like that for the rest of the gig.

But somehow he didn't hear the cheers, or feel the love, so after the show, he told me, "I told you I'm not no piano player."

I said, "Man, didn't you hear those folks?"

"What folks?" he asked.

"The audience! They loved you!"

"They did? But I'm not no piano player."

"Ronnie, I've played with the greatest piano players of our day. I played with Herbie Hancock, Chick Corea, all those cats, and I'm not gonna lie to you—you're not there yet. But trust me, there ain't nothing wrong with your piano playing, *nothing*. You're gonna join my band, right?" After several more minutes of flattery and cajoling, Ronnie couldn't refuse, and he was doubly happy when I hired Stanley Banks, one of his best friends, to play bass. (Stanley has been with me more or less since.) Once we got a few rehearsals under our belts, we sounded good, man, really, really good. But something was missing.

The prior year, I was at Buddy Rich's nightclub on the East Side of New York, checking out a band led by Bernard "Pretty" Purdie, one of the funkiest drummers you'll ever hear. His piano player, a kid from Argentina named Jorge Dalto, was as dynamic as any keyboardist I'd heard in recent memory, so I had him write down his phone number on a napkin; I stuck it in my coat pocket, where it stayed for many, many months. I forgot about the napkin, but I never forgot about Jorge.

Now Ronnie, for as good of a player as he was, was unpredictable—for instance, if he was having a bad night, he'd quit in the middle of the show, then come back for the second set—so I thought I'd better cover myself and bring another keyboardist into the fold, figuring that one day, Ronnie would quit in the middle of a show and never come back. Plus, simply put, a second keyboard would sound *baaaaad*. So I invited Jorge to jam with the band: "Come on over here, man," I insisted. "Come to one of our rehearsals. This isn't anything serious. We're just gonna have some fun. Let's see what happens."

Now Jorge had never heard Ronnie play, and he, like most everybody else, was blown away. Before he even touched the keys, Jorge said, "I can't play with your band."

I said, "Why?"

"Why?" He pointed at Ronnie. "This kid. He's a bitch, man."

"I know what he can do, Jorge, but he's not you. Y'all don't play the same things. He's different than you." It took another half hour of talking, but finally, Jorge sat down and got busy, and it was the most incredible thing, so incredible that I took them both on the road. And folks thought I was crazy.

See, aside from Miles Davis's group with Keith Jarrett and Chick Corea—and, maybe Ferrante and Teicher—two piano players in one jazz band was practically unheard of. (A few years later, Chick Corea and Herbie Hancock did a tour together, but it always remained a rarity.) Not only did I have these two *baaaaad* keyboardists, but they both played every keyboard on the planet. Ronnie was a phenomenal synthesizer player, in part because organs and synths required a similar touch, and he knew organs; and Jorge played some mean Rhodes and an equally mean acoustic piano. (I also had Jorge on Clavinet, an electric keyboard with a distinct, funky, almost percussive sound that Stevie Wonder had used to great effect. Stevie used the Clavinet instead of a rhythm guitar on "Superstition," and everybody dug that, so I had Jorge do the same thing.)

We were opening up for somebody during our first week on the road with Ronnie and Jorge, and it was special—so special that after our set, about 80 percent of the audience left, figuring that the headliner wouldn't match up to the supporting act. For the next few months, that happened on a regular basis, and the word started to get out: *Don't hire George Benson's band to open for you, because you can't follow them.* Yeah, word got out to everybody, even my old friend Herbie Hancock.

Herbie had offered me a shocking amount of money to bring my band on the road with his. (I'm not going to name figures. Suffice it to say that when he told me the number, I darn near dropped the phone, then, after I hung up, convinced myself that I'd be wealthy for the rest of my life.) But a week before we were to hit the road, they canceled us.

But still no *big* record . . . or at least that's what I was led to believe. As far as I knew, come 1976, our CTI records—*Beyond the Blue Horizon*, *White Rabbit*, *Body Talk*, *Bad Benson*, *Good King Bad*, and a nice little session I co-led with Joe Farrell called *Benson & Farrell*—had sold a few copies here and there. But it turned out that it might've been considerably more than a few, because Creed Taylor, for reasons that were never made clear to anybody, wasn't able to give us accurate sales figures . . . but it also might've been considerably less than a few, because CTI's distribution system wasn't nearly as powerful as that of a major label's. Finally, after some digging, we found out that *Bad Benson*—a quintet date featuring Ron Carter and pianist Kenny Barron, my jazziest session for CTI—sold over 100,000 copies.

The funk, the soul, the jazz/funk, and the jazz/soul was fulfilling on every level, but I'd never be able to abandon good ol' garden variety straight-up jazz, even if I wanted to—which I most definitely didn't. And even though the general public didn't think of me as a bebop or swing player, those folks who knew me well were aware that I not only had the ability to play straight-ahead but *craved* it. And one of those folks was John Hammond.

In the autumn of 1975, John gave me a call with some news: "You know that TV show *Soundstage*?" he asked.

"Sure, man. Everybody knows *Soundstage*. Well, at least hip people know *Soundstage*." *Soundstage*, a PBS show that originated out of Chicago, was a simple concept: Once every week or so, a musical act took its unadorned stage and played for an hour. Dizzy played it, Professor Longhair played it, Al Green played it, Muddy Waters played it. It was an incredibly important show, because not everybody out there would ever have had the opportunity to see these cats live, in concert. So thanks to PBS, you didn't have to go to the cats—the cats came to you.

"Well," John said, "they want to do this silly tribute to me, or something. I don't know why." That was John, modest to a fault. "They want me to get in touch with people I've worked with, and I'm getting in touch with you."

I was speechless. The list of John's associates is a mile and a half long, filled with the biggest of the big—heck, if you'd have asked me, I wouldn't have even guessed I was on the list. "I'm in. Whatever you want me to do, I'll do. Just tell me what, when, and where."

"Okay, then, let's talk about Charlie Christian."

I said, "Man, you know I'll talk about Charlie Christian anytime, anyplace, anywhere."

"Great. So you know I've always thought you could be the second coming of Charlie . . ."

Interrupting, I said, "Don't even try that. Charlie is first, second, and third, all the way up to a millionth. We've discussed this."

John chuckled. "Okay, okay, okay, but even if you're not the second coming of Charlie Christian, you can pull that stuff off, so I want you to play on the special."

"That would be my honor."

"You'll have a great time. We're also getting Red Norvo to play vibes, and Papa Jo Jones on drums, and Benny Carter to play alto, and Benny Morton on trombone, and Teddy Wilson on piano, and Milt Hinton on bass. And you're all gonna play this Basie thing called, 'I May Be Wrong, It's John's Idea.'"

"I'm in, man."

"Great, great, great." He paused. "There's one other thing."

"Yeah?"

"You'll be playing with Benny Goodman. And you'll be performing some of the music of the Benny Goodman Sextet . . ."

"Cool."

". . . with Benny Goodman."

"*What?*" I darn near dropped the phone. Between 1939 and 1941, Benny led a six-piece band that practically redefined jazz, mostly because Charlie Christian was in the house. Benny was a swing clarinetist, and Charlie was a bebop guitarist, and the musical tension between the edgy guitarist and the traditionalists who made up the rest of the group was palpable. And that's what made the whole thing so exciting: You've got five cats playing conservatively over a *chunk-chunk-chunk-chunk* swing beat, then you've got this other cat playing newfangled lines with a jagged, hop-skip feel. Most every one of their tunes—"Seven Come Eleven," "A Smo-o-o-o-oth One," "Flying Home"—was a perfect three-minute symphony, a microcosm of the transition that helped lead us where we are now. "I darn sure want to play with Benny, but are you sure he wants to play with me?"

"Well, I've been trying to convince him that you're the next Charlie Christian . . ."

"And?"

"And he keeps telling me there isn't another Charlie Christian."

"Yeah, he's right," I said. "But that's not really a good sign, is it?" Suddenly, I got nervous, because Benny Goodman has a reputation for being a tyrant and a bit of a jerk. There were stories of him yelling at the cats in his band onstage; stealing reeds from the other clarinet players in his group; and underpaying his sidemen, then ditching them at a restaurant, leaving them to cover the bill. I could only imagine how he'd treat a young guy who'd been compared to one of his greatest musical associates.

John said, "Don't worry about it, George. Mentality-wise, he's stuck in the 1930s and 1940s, but he doesn't mean any harm. Just play your butt off like I know you can, and you'll be fine."

The taping wasn't for a few weeks, which gave me plenty of extra time to get even more nervous. I'd played with some heavy cats, but those cats were my contemporaries, guys my own age who spoke my language, both verbally and musically. Put me on *Soundstage* with Miles Davis, Thelonious Monk, and John Coltrane, and I'd be cool. But with the likes of Benny Carter, Teddy Wilson, and Papa Jo Jones, I was out of my element. Not only that, but I was an outsider—those guys had known one another for years, and I was the new kid in class. I prayed the music would bring us together.

It did. From the get-go, there was no attitude, no drama, and no discomfort—only a mutual respect and a shared desire to pay proper homage to John, a gentleman whom we all loved and revered.

Okay, maybe there *was* a little bit of drama.

As noted previously, Benny Goodman had a well-earned reputation as a musical tyrant, a man who ruled his band—and every band with whom he performed—with an iron fist. Even though this was a one-off TV show, and even though the show was meant to honor a mutual friend and respected colleague, the other cats in the group were frightened to make any decisions, to do anything on their own. During rehearsal, they all stood there quietly, waiting until Benny told them what to do, waiting for the infamous Benny Goodman Signal. (Sometimes Benny liked to go off-script, meaning that if he wanted to take an unscheduled solo, he'd chop his hand like Bruce Lee, and when he made that gesture, you'd better shut up, get low, and stay in the background, because it was Benny Goodman time. But I didn't know that law.) Me, once I saw the lights, the cameras, and John Hammond, I got over my nerves. I was there to make John proud and to resurrect the spirit of Charlie Christian.

The taping flew by in a blur of swinging solos and good vibes, and before I knew it, Benny was counting off the last number of the set, "Seven Come Eleven," probably the most famous tune in the Goodman/Christian discography. Up until then, the spirit of Charlie Christian was sitting next to me on a stool similar to mine, but when Benny and I started playing the intro lick, Charlie borrowed my fingers.

After Benny played his solo—and his solo was *baaaaad*, man—it was my turn. Charlie used my fingers to play one of his licks, then I took over and did one of my own. That went on for a few phrases, then a few more, then a few more after that. I noticed that John was smiling and snapping with a sense of joy and enthusiasm that I remembered from when he used to hear me gig at Minton's Playhouse.

I blasted through a couple of choruses—or should I say Charlie and I blasted through a couple of choruses—at which point, I got the Benny Goodman Signal. But here's the thing: I still didn't know the Benny Goodman Signal. So I kept right on playing. Out of the corner of my eye, I saw Teddy Wilson staring at me with a look that was part horror and part joy, and it seemed like he started hitting the piano a bit harder. The rest of the band followed suit, and the energy jumped to a higher level . . . at which point I received my second Benny Goodman Signal, which, again, I didn't heed. The band went crazy, the energy amped up even further, and John Hammond, well, he went to the moon.

I thought to myself, *Man, these cats are digging me! I must be playing one heckuva solo.* But that wasn't really it. Sure, they liked what I was doing, but they were more excited that I'd defied their tormentor.

I guess Benny was less of a tyrant than he used to be, because rather than get angry, he started improvising right alongside me, interweaving his lines with my own, and even though it was nothing we'd planned, it flat-out swung as if we'd rehearsed it for hours, because Benny Goodman was the King of Swing. As the applause and appreciation of the small studio audience washed over us, I thought, *If I never do anything else in my life, I'll still be happy.*

A few weeks after the show, Benny had me up to his apartment to rehearse. (Benny, it turned out, rehearsed his band all the darn time—other than music, it often seemed like Benny had no life—and he rode them hard. But that's why he was so good at what he did.) When I arrived, he was noodling around on his clarinet. And he kept noodling. And noodling. And noodling. Some five minutes later, he gave me an appraising look and said, "Oh. Are you here?"

I tried to stay cool. "I am. And I'm ready to work!"

"Can you play 'Gilly'?"

"Gilly" was one of the lesser-known gems from the Goodman/ Christian sessions, but I knew it . . . sort of. "Yeah, yeah, yeah, I think I can do that. How do you want me to play it?" I asked.

"Play it like it's written," he sneered.

I said, "I don't read music."

His face got all red, and for a second, I thought he was going to wrap his clarinet around my throat. But then he counted off the tune, and we jammed on it for a good long while, and it felt *great*.

I finished up the song with a flourish, after which he nodded and said, "You know what? I'm gonna fire Bucky and hire you." Bucky was Bucky Pizzarelli, Benny's regular guitarist. He'd been playing with Benny for years, and was one of the music's finest living swing guitarists.

"You can't fire Bucky," I said. "He's *baaaaad*. Besides, I couldn't play with you all the time, anyhow. I can only do it when I'm not doing anything with my band. I can't put those guys out of work." What I didn't say was, *Plus, you make me kind of nervous.*

"Well, why don't you come out on the road with me for a couple of weeks. Maybe it'll be a good fit. Maybe you'll like it. Maybe you'll want to hop aboard." We checked our schedules, and he had two weeks' worth of gigs that coincided with an empty slot in my calendar, so I hopped aboard.

The gigs were enjoyable, but certainly not enough that I'd be willing to set aside everything I'd worked so hard for over the last three years. Benny, however, thought that joining him for two weeks meant I'd be joining him forever.

When his manager called with a list of upcoming gigs, I said, "Wait a minute. I only signed up for half a month. It was great, but I'm done."

She growled, "Benson, if you mess Benny Goodman up, you will never play another union gig again."

I cracked up. "I ain't in no union now. I ain't been in the union in eight years. They kicked me out, and I stayed out." (I've since gone back in, and the union has actually been quite good to me. It enabled me to get benefits for both myself and my band, and on one memorable instance, I went to pick up a $500 check and left with about $8,000 for past gigs.)

We ended up making a record together—and a good one, at that—but our relationship was always a bit frosty. But soon before he passed away in 1986, we mended fences at another tribute to John Hammond, this one being a concert at Lincoln Center in New York. We shared the stage with another Hammond discovery, blues guitarist Stevie Ray Vaughan, and it turned out to be a nice night of music, which washed away any bad vibes. I have nothing but good memories of Benny Goodman. He lived up to everything I had thought he was going to be, and more.

Interlude #4

Chops vs. Vibes

When Wynton Marsalis took over the trumpet chair in Art Blakey's Jazz Messengers in 1980, jazz folks were blown away that this bespectacled teenager from New Orleans knew the musical language so well; that he could fluently speak Miles Davis, Lee Morgan, and Freddie Hubbard; and that he could play really, really fast. Within a year or two, the backlash started, and these same folks were saying that Wynton was all chops and no soul, that his playing was all about speed and not about warmth.

I don't know if Wynton took this all to heart, but over the next several years, he made several albums that showed off his softer side, then, not too long thereafter, started incorporating a Louis Armstrong vibe into his repertoire, and while Armstrong had plenty of technique, he was all about feel. Wynton eventually found a perfect balance between chops and vibe; little wonder that he's one of our country's greatest jazz ambassadors. I've known him since he was thirteen, and he's just a down-home person who happens to be a genius.

But here's the thing: We've got the technicians over here, and we've got the soulful artists over there, and too often, never the twain shall meet. The speedsters and the soulsters both belong in the same category—jazz—but just because they approach it from different points of view, some observers take the segregation route: separate and unequal.

Having said that, I think that if you want to be the best cat you can be—and if you'd like to reach the widest possible audience—do both. Play with both technique and heart. Walk and chew gum. Take everything into consideration. Go the extra mile. Your horizons will expand to the point that you'll go over the moon.

Consider this: If you're all chops, you might find yourself meandering around the tune, with no place to go. You might speed yourself into a corner, with no way to escape and nothing to say. On the other hand, if you're all feel, you might have a brilliant idea to share with the world, but you lack the linguistic skills that would enable you to get the brilliant idea out of your head and into your hands. You owe it to your audience to learn the language and speak it properly.

If you want to know how to straddle technique and soul, buy yourself about fifty Gene Ammons records. Gene—who was known to friends and fans as Jug—was a tenor sax player from Chicago who came to prominence in the mid-1940s, during the bebop-to-swing transition era. Unlike the majority of the cats on the scene at that point, Gene didn't choose a side. He didn't play bop. He didn't play swing. He played jazz. He played music.

Jug blew everybody away, because his harmonies and rhythms related to one another in an accessible manner, thus making it easier for his audience to relate. Technique-wise, he wasn't Charlie Parker or Dizzy Gillespie—nobody was Charlie Parker or Dizzy Gillespie— but he had enough in his arsenal to be able to say what he needed to say. One of the many, many cool things about Jug was that over his two-plus decades of recording as a leader, he played in most every kind of jazz setting you can imagine, for example: Blue Gene (1958) is a straight-up bebop jam session; Bad Bossa Nova (1962) is, as you might suspect, a nice little Latin record; and Big Bad Jug (1972) is gutbucket electric funk. But on each of these records, Gene Ammons sounds like Gene Ammons: fast enough to convey the soul, and soulful enough to make the soul agreeable. (This approach doesn't just apply to improvised music. Classical artists can also fall prey to being all fast notes or all naked emotion. But man, Andrés Segovia, he could do it all. He never put in too much, and he never left anything out.)

Since pop and rock became America's dominant forms of popular music in the late 1950s and early 1960s, jazz's biggest enemy has been its lack of exposure. I can't tell you how many times somebody has pulled me aside and said, "George, what are we going to do for jazz? How can we get more people to listen? How can we get more people to buy our records? How can we get more people to go to the concerts? How can we keep the music alive?"

The answer is simple: Make people want to give jazz more exposure, which can be accomplished by putting our best jazz cats forward and making sure that if somebody goes to a jazz gig, he or she will be treated to an evening of heartfelt melodies delivered with a high level of technical proficiency. To paraphrase the title of Ray Charles's album produced by my friend Quincy Jones, Jazz + Soul = Genius.

8 From *Breezin'* to Broadway and Beyond

For jazz cats like me, the 1960s made sense. You'd cut your album for Prestige or Blue Note or Riverside or Contemporary or Pacific or—if you were really lucky—Capitol or Columbia. Your record would get released, you'd go on the road for a few months, then you'd go home and, assuming your record sold a few thousand copies, start the cycle again. In between, you'd pick up a sideman gig, or take to the road with somebody else's band. You made a living, you made music, and you had fun.

In the 1970s, things changed because the definition of jazz changed. In, say, 1964, if you went to a jazz club, you knew you'd most likely be getting a quartet, a quintet, or a sextet playing a typical head-solos-head format over a few original compositions and a few standards. Each set lasted about an hour, and each set had a beginning, a middle, and an end. It was comfortable. Come the mid-1970s, jazz's horizons had, to say the least, expanded. You had jazz-rock and jazz fusion, jazz-rock-fusion and soul-jazz, avant-garde and avant-bop, and this and that and so on. For us musicians, it opened up a world of possibilities and opportunities: One day I might be in the studio backed with strings, singing a Sinatra tune, and the next I'm sharing the stage with Phil Upchurch and Eric Gale, playing a slow blues for twenty minutes.

For jazz listeners, however, it was a different story. From the mid-1970s to the early 1980s, the jazz that I grew up on was off of most people's radars, and I think that might have had to do with the fact that fans didn't know what they'd be getting from one record to the next, or from one concert to another. Also, what with the ease of purchasing and playing synthesizers and other newfangled electric instruments, tastes and attitudes were evolving, sometimes for the good and sometimes for the not so good.

This is why jazz record labels were dropping like flies; Prestige, Blue Note, CTI, and their brethren had drastically cut the number of their releases, gone on hiatus, or pulled the plug altogether. This left musicians with fewer and fewer venues in which to record, and it started to seem that in terms of advances, it was all or nothing.

I was done with CTI, so I was a guy in search of a label. Thus, the word went out.

A gentleman who shall remain nameless—even all these years later—called me up and said, "George, the conversation we're having right now is between you and me." He was practically whispering.

"Okay."

"There's a guy."

"Yeah."

"His name is Nesuhi Ertegün."

"Right."

"You ever hear of him?"

"I know *Ahmet* Ertegün." Ahmet founded Atlantic Records. Everybody knew Ahmet Ertegün.

"Well, Nesuhi is his brother. He's in charge of WEA International." WEA International was the worldwide arm of Warner Bros./ Elektra/Atlantic, aka WEA, arguably the largest record conglomerate in the world—home, at that point, to such acts as the Rolling Stones, Fleetwood Mac, the Eagles, and Linda Ronstadt. Its back catalog wasn't anything to sneeze at, either.

"What about him?" I asked.

He paused. The silence went on and on, to the point that I was going to hang up. Finally, my friend said, "They're going to make you a big offer."

"That's crazy, man," I said. "They don't do jazz, as far as I know."

"Listen, all I heard is that they're going to come to you, and they're going to make you a big offer, and it's going to be over a million dollars."

"*What?* That don't sound right." And it didn't. Here's me, a cat whose best-selling record might or might not have moved 100,000 copies. And there's WEA, a company who made its money on gold- and platinum-record-earning rock groups. How *could* that sound right? "Somebody's pulling your leg, or you're getting some bad information, or . . ."

"Listen," he interrupted, "I know this doesn't sound right to you, but trust me, in the next few days you're gonna hear something. And when you do, act surprised."

"Um, okay."

"And no matter what, promise me you won't tell anybody where you got this information from."

"I promise." And that's a promise I've kept.

A few nights later, we were gigging at Keystone Korner in San Francisco, one of the new breed of jazz clubs that wasn't tied to a specific jazz style. The owner, Todd Barkan, would hire my funky, loud, two-keyboard band one week, then Cedar Walton's pretty acoustic piano trio the next. It was right next to the local police station; Freddie always used to say, "We're at the Keystone Korner this week, right next to the Keystone Kops." As had fortunately—*very* fortunately—been the case over the last few years, the club was packed for our gig, with lines around the corner. We were backstage, getting ready to go on—I was hunched over my guitar, doing some final tuning up—when I felt a tap on my shoulder. "Mr. Benson?"

I turned around, and there stood an olive-skinned Caucasian gentleman with perfectly combed hair; a serious, almost grim expression; and a jacket on which was plastered a Bugs Bunny graphic. I thought, *Uh-oh. What's up, doc?* "Can I help you?"

"Yeah. Who's your manager? What number can I call to get in touch with him?"

"Um, can I ask why?"

He stuck out his hand. "Bob Krasnow, WEA International."

We shook hands, then I said, "We gotta go play. But, man, I wanna talk to you after the set. Cool?"

Bob flicked a piece of dust off the lapel of his Bugs Bunny jacket and said, "Cool."

When we finished up the set, Bob and I chatted until the break was over. We swapped James Brown stories—he was a white guy, but he loved, respected, and knew black music as well as anybody—after which he said, "I want to talk to your manager. I want to work out something between you and Warner Bros. Records. I want you on our label, and I want you there for a long time."

I played it cool. "Okay, man. We'll try to work it out." But deep down in my heart and my gut, I was thrilled.

So I called up Jimmy Boyd first thing in the morning. "Listen, this guy came to see me last night, and his name is Bob Krasnow, and he's from Warner Bros., and this other guy—and I can't tell you who—told me last week that Warners is gonna make me a huge offer, and . . ." I went on in that vein for a few more minutes.

When I finally ran out of breath, Jimmy said, "Man, don't believe all this stuff. Nobody's paying no jazz cat nothin'. Heck, Grover Washington Jr. sold 750,000 records, and he didn't make any money at all, and nobody from no place like Warner Bros. offered him a deal." Grover was a soulful saxophonist out of Philadelphia, and his last album, *Mr. Magic*—which he cut for Kudu Records, another one of Creed Taylor's labels—was a massive hit. It even climbed onto the

Billboard 200 albums chart, and jazz records—even jazz records with a deep R&B vibe—never charted on *Billboard*. *Never.*

"But Bob said he wanted me on his label!"

"It was probably just talk, and if it wasn't just talk, it probably won't be for much bread."

I said, "Isn't it possible that somebody loves me enough to offer me a decent record deal?"

"Anything's possible, George. But don't get your hopes up. It might be a bunch of jive."

"Maybe. But will you call him?"

Jimmy said, "Maybe."

Man, for the next week, I called Jimmy five times a day, asking if or when he'd gotten in touch with Bob, and he kept telling me, "Sounds like a bunch of jive to me."

So finally I took matters into my own hands and called Bob myself.

"This is unexpected," he said. "I thought I'd be hearing from your manager."

"My manager doesn't believe it."

"Doesn't believe what?" Bob asked.

"Doesn't believe that you want to sign me."

"*What?* Listen, you tell your manager that I want you, I want George Benson, on this record label, and I mean *yesterday*! I don't care what it takes! *This is happening!*"

I felt Bob's voice thundering through the phone line. Not heard, mind you—*felt*. I thought, *Man, I'm glad this cat is on my side.*

Jimmy and I went to California to sign the contract and get our advance, and they gave us a check, right then and there, something not done by all record labels. Jimmy pointed at the check and asked, "Where's this bank at?"

The Warner people gave him a funny look, then said, "Across the street. Why?"

He said, "Don't worry about it," then we practically sprinted across the street and cashed that thing. See, we didn't trust anybody, man, not after what we'd been through. I gave Jimmy his 10 percent cut right away, then put the rest in my pocket. I felt secure, successful, and financially comfortable, something I'd never dreamed would happen. I mean, I'm the guy who'd thought that if I ever had $10,000 to my name, I'd retire. We went back to New York that night; then, as soon as I possibly could, I moved my family out of the Bronx and bought a beautiful home in New Jersey, and was even able to put a little in the bank. Secure, successful, and financially comfortable.

The only thing I had to do now was to make this record. And we only had four days to do it.

When I first started going into studios, we'd be lucky if we had two days. Some labels got the cats together and told them, "You have the studio from 9:00 a.m. to 5:00 p.m., and we need to get three records out of you. See you tomorrow. And don't be late." Other labels gave the artists a tiny bit of time to prepare, then a bit more time to record. (There was an old joke that went like this: What's the difference between a Prestige record and a Blue Note record? Answer: One day of rehearsal. Whether or not that's true is up for debate, but nobody will argue that most of those old Blue Notes sound tighter than most of those old Prestiges.) I had more studio time for my Verve sessions, and even more than that with my A&Ms and CTIs, but that was out of necessity; it's one thing to cut a handful of blues-based tunes with McDuff, Holloway, and Dukes, because we toured nonstop, and the tunes were straight up and no frills, and it's another to play brand-new material arranged by some cat you've never met, backed by a big band or a string section. Those sessions sometimes took a week or two, which felt like an eternity.

Come 1976, there were numerous factors that made things a bit more complicated, the primary one being the proper equalization and mixing of electronic instruments. If your band is sax, guitar, organ, and drums, the engineer will know exactly what to do, and he'll do it *fast*—you'll set up, you'll plug in, you'll do a soundcheck, then *boom*, eight tunes, two takes each, and home for dinner and a shower, then off to Minton's or the Vanguard for three sets. But now, bands had all kinds of different instrumentation, and even if they had similar instrumentation, they might be looking for a different sound, and not only a different sound as a band but a different sound on each tune. To get a song or an album just right, you couldn't just plug in and go—you had to take your time, to let things breathe, to see what the room sounded like, and so on. There were a lot of logistical factors involved in making a contemporary album, and in a perfect world, you'd get a lot of time. And four days is most definitely *not* a lot of time, especially if you want to live up to high expectations and justify the biggest advance you've ever received in your life.

Now I don't know if it was the pressure or the adrenaline but we got that thing done *quick*. We rehearsed for one day, then recorded for three, and we only needed the three because we nailed everything in one or two takes. For instance, "This Masquerade," a cover of a tune by singer/songwriter Leon Russell—which had already been recorded by the Carpenters and Helen Reddy—was done in a single take, and I never in a million years would've thought it would make any noise on *Billboard*. (Confession time: Our producer, Tommy LiPuma, sent me "This Masquerade" a bunch of times, trying to convince me to cut it, and I didn't even check it out because I didn't know anything about Leon Russell. Finally, when we were in the studio, he cornered me and said, "George, what do you think about that song?"

"What song?"

" 'This Masquerade.' "

Before I could tell him I hadn't listened to it yet, Jorge Dalto said, "Oh, that's my favorite song. That's Leon Russell. He's *baaaaad*."

I just stared at him, thinking, *How can Jorge know more about the music business than me?* Then I thought, *If this Leon Russell is such a star, how come I don't know him?* And then I thought, *Maybe*

I better learn this song. Turns out, "This Masquerade" is one of the finest tunes of our time, with a beautiful melody and a great story. Plus, I found out later that it's based on the jazz standard "Angel Eyes," which is why so many jazz musicians dig playing it, whether they're approaching it as pop or bop. Leon did us all a great favor when he wrote it.)

One of the reasons the music flowed so well is that everybody involved with the project was happy, and one of the reasons everybody was so happy was that the sessions were truly collaborative—and not just between our band but between me and the engineer, Al Schmitt. Al had been producing and engineering albums forever—okay, not exactly *forever* but since the late 1950s—and had a wealth of diverse experience. He'd worked with jazz cats like Cal Tjader, Al Hirt, and Rosemary Clooney; soul cats like Sam Cooke and Dr. John; and rock cats like Neil Young and Jackson Browne, so he knew how to straddle styles. And he worked *with* us, not *against* us. It's not that Creed Taylor and I were adversaries or anything; it's just that I couldn't make any comments about his studio techniques without it becoming a thing. But with Al, if you wanted to try it, he'd try it.

For example, during the playback of "This Masquerade," I told him, "There's something about this vocal I'm not digging. I never liked the sound of my voice. It's got too much low end in it. It saturates the tape, and it takes away from all the other instruments."

Nodding, he said, "I feel you. We can do something about that, man, no problem." Then he clicked a few hertz off of the bottom end. And *wow*, there it was, the sound I'd been hearing in my head but had never heard through the speakers.

"That's a *lot* better," I said, probably giving him a big, silly grin. "Maybe some more?" *Click*, a few more hertz. "Oh, that's a lot better! Can you do some more?"

He scratched his chin and furrowed his brow, then slowly said, "I don't want to go too far, George. It's gonna get skinny in a minute. Your voice is so rich and buttery that I don't want to dilute it."

"Just one more click, Al. Please."

"Okay," he said, then *click*.

When I heard it, I almost passed out, I was so happy. "That's what I think I sound like," I said. "When I'm singing, that's the George Benson I hear. Up until now, whenever I heard my recordings, they'd be rumbling at the bottom, like *rrrrrrrrrrrrrrrrrrrrrrr*. But now, Al, now the EQ is *perfect*." And that's the way things should be. Everybody should be on the same page: the leader, the sidemen, the engineer, and the producer. And in this case, the producer wasn't just on the same page—the producer was writing a book.

I'd met Tommy LiPuma a few times when I was with A&M, where he was a staff producer. I always thought he was a nice, knowledgeable cat, but we never worked together because he wasn't handling the jazz stuff; he took lesser-known artists, like the Sandpipers and Chris Montez, and helped them become stars. Soon he moved from A&M to Blue Thumb, where he started taking to the studio with jazz cats like Joe Sample and the Crusaders, vocalist Ben Sidran, South African trumpeter Hugh Masekela, and Hungarian guitarist Gábor Szabó. He made a mainstream name for himself in 1974, when he worked on the soundtrack to *The Way We Were* with Barbra Streisand; thanks to the album's creative and sales success, he landed a gig as one of Warner Bros.'s house producers.

Like all successful record producers, Tommy had a great ear and was willing to veer off course in order to make the best record possible. (Matter of fact, he was the first producer who wanted to focus on my vocals.) But what raised him to the next level was that he had an encyclopedic memory, something that came in handy when it came to picking material. Soon before we started cutting the album, Tommy reached into his computer of a brain and suggested that we cut a tune called *Breezin'*, a composition that was cowritten by soul singer Bobby Womack and Tommy's old friend Gábor Szabó.

Tommy pulled out Gábor's album *High Contrast*, dropped the needle on track one, and within a few bars I could see why he thought it would be a nice tune for me. The guitar line was melodic, soulful, and simple, and the medium-tempo, churning groove would allow me the opportunity to play some hot double-time licks, some Wes Montgomery octaves, and a whole bunch of pretty stuff. After we listened to it a second time through, I said, "What's the use of doing another version of this? This one sounds great. What would I do to improve on it?" Before he could answer, something dawned on me: "What we need is a new idea, something fresh. If we can get Bobby Womack to come in, maybe he can give us something new."

I'd never met Bobby, but I knew his music, and that cat was *baaaaad*. He wasn't a crossover star, but folks who knew his music dug the heck out of him. With tunes like "Lookin' for a Love," "Woman's Gotta Have It," and "That's the Way I Feel About Cha," how could you *not* dig him? I had a gut feeling he could provide that special something that would make it worth our while to cover his tune. Tommy agreed, so we invited him over.

When Bobby arrived the next day, we were listening to the playback of "This Masquerade," and before we even said hello, he said, "Hey, man, who the heck is that voice coming out of?"

Tommy said, "That's George Benson."

"*What?*" Bobby said. "But I thought he was a guitar player."

"Yeah, he's a guitar player," Al said, "but he also sings."

Bobby just nodded; then, after we listened to "This Masquerade" again—about which Tommy said, "George, we could do a million takes of this, but that song will never get better than that"—he told us the story behind "Breezin'."

"Believe it or not, we just threw it together at the end of the recording session. It was like a jam tune. But Gábor was good at that stuff, you know, what with his folksy style, simple but jazzy. He didn't think the song was going to be anything because it was so simple—to him, it was just *do-re-mi-fa-sol-la-ti-do*, so he took his name off of it."

I said, "But you still dig it, right?"

"Yeah, but there was something I wanted to do on the track, but it never made it onto the record."

"What's that?"

And then he sang me the opening lick, and man, what a lick it was. I knew if we played it just right—right tempo, right feel, right sound—that people would go nuts. I mentally patted myself on the back for coming up with the idea to bring Bobby into Capitol Records Studios.

On the fourth day of the session, we just hung out and listened to the tracks, confident that we had everything we needed, happy as can be, dreaming of *possibilities*. The possibility of hitting the *Billboard* charts hard like Grover Washington Jr. . . . . The possibility of playing theaters and auditoriums . . . The possibility of touring Europe and Asia . . . The possibility of not being dropped from the label before we got the chance to cut a second record. And believe me, in 1976, there was no guarantee you'd have the opportunity to make a follow-up—after all, the music business was and is a very what-have-you-done-for-me-lately kind of industry.

Tommy called me up the next day, practically out of breath. "Listen, George, I took this record to the Warner Bros. suits. I burst uninvited into one of their pow-wows and said, 'Cut this. Cut this meeting.'"

I said, "*Whaaaaaaaaaaat?*"

"Yeah, there were fifteen or twenty cats sitting around this big oval table. 'Cut the meeting,' I said. One of the guys asked, 'What's going on, Tommy?' And I told him, 'I've got something. You've got to hear this.' And then I had one of my engineers bring in a whole sound system."

"Wait, you had a cat waiting out in the hallway with speakers and stuff?"

"If you're gonna do it, you gotta do it right."

"I can't argue with that," I said.

"So once it was set up, I put on 'This Masquerade,' and their jaws all hit the table. One of the guys said, 'Who's that?' and I told him it was you. Another one of the guys said, 'I thought he was a guitar player.' I said, 'He is, but he also sings.' Another guy said, 'Get that record. I want to hear the rest of it.' I said, 'I'm still working on it, but check this out,' and then I put on 'Breezin'.' Another of the guys said, 'When are we going to get that record? We need to release it *yesterday*.' He was practically yelling, man. I told him there's something else I wanted to do before we put it to bed."

I said, "There is?" Nobody'd mentioned anything else about doing something else.

"There is," Tommy said.

"What's that?"

"*Strings.*"

Who was I to say no to an orchestra? "Sounds good to me, man."

So Tommy took that record—on which we'd spent peanuts—and hopped a plane to Europe, where he got in touch with an old friend of his, Claus Ogerman, a gentleman with whom I was quite familiar; after all, he'd written string arrangements for the likes of Frank Sinatra, pianist Bill Evans, and, most important of all to me, Wes Montgomery. *Tequila*, the record on which Claus worked with Wes, was one of the most successful of his career. If he did right by Wes, I was sure he'd do right by me.

Tommy met Claus in Germany, where they went into the studio with the Munich Symphony Orchestra, and the sessions started out on a bad note. Here's the thing: When an orchestra lays overdubs, it's essential that they're able to hear exactly what's coming through the tape. Sure, they can watch the conductor for the tempo, but if they can't hear what it is they're accompanying, it becomes difficult to lock down the proper feel, so it's crucial that each and every musician has a set of headphones.

The studio in Munich had twenty earphones. The orchestra in Munich had sixty people.

Tommy freaked out for a few minutes but then came up with an idea: no headphones for anybody other than the conductor. That was the greatest thing that could've happened. These cats, Germany's best of the best, did what orchestral musicians do best: They watched the conductor, and the music floated. They made a bed for me that made my guitar sound like it was coming from heaven above. Tommy was thrilled beyond belief . . . that is, until they threw him out of the studio. See, he didn't buy enough time to finish the tracks, so he hopped over to England and recruited the London Symphony Orchestra to complete the record. What with all the travel, the hotels, the high-end restaurants—Tommy eats at only the finest restaurants in the world—the Munich studio time, and the London studio time, we spent more on recording the strings than we did on the rest of the album. *Considerably* more. There were a few numbers people at WEA who weren't happy.

But as soon as *Breezin'* hit the streets, all that negativity went right out the window. For that matter, even *before* it hit the streets, thanks to the fine folks at WRVR.

WRVR was one of the few jazz radio stations in New York, so I made it a point to maintain a good relationship with them, to stop by and visit, to always be available for interviews, to just generally be a nice guy. When I received the *Breezin'* test pressing, I figured it would be a good idea to cruise by the station and let them have a listen. Warner Bros. was buzzing about the album, so it couldn't hurt.

They put me on the air first thing in the morning, and the deejay asked, "What are you working on, George? What's new and exciting?"

"Well, it just so happens that I brought along a test pressing of my new record. It's not gonna be available until next week, but maybe we can play one track."

"Okay," he said, "but only one track. Here's the title cut to George Benson's forthcoming album, *Breezin'*. Enjoy."

Apparently listeners enjoyed, because all the lights on all the telephones in the studio lit up: *Click click click click click click click click click click*. Staring at the blinking phones, the deejay said, "Wow, that's a great record, George," then he answered a few of the calls. Right before the cut was finished, he said, "All these people want to talk to you."

I said, "What the heck do they want to talk to me about?" I'd never spoken to a listener during a radio interview, in part because no listeners had ever expressed interest in speaking to me.

"The record," he said.

"Can I just talk about it with you?"

He nodded, then fired up his mic. "That was 'Breezin'" by Mr. George Benson. I have George in the studio with me. Can you tell us when the record's coming out?"

"Next Tuesday." And that's all I said. For some reason, I suddenly got all shy.

"And can you tell us a little bit more about the album?"

"Um, well, it has six cuts, and I had Jorge Dalto and Ronnie Foster playing keyboards, and Phil Upchurch playing rhythm guitar, and Ralph McDonald and Harvey Mason playing drums, and Stanley Banks playing bass, and Claus Ogerman did the string arrangements, and I played guitar and sang a little bit."

"You sang? What did you sing?"

"This song by Leon Russell," I said.

The deejay looked mildly shocked. "You mean Leon Russell the pop singer/songwriter?"

"The very same. It's called 'This Masquerade.' Can we play it?"

"We sure can," he said, then dropped the needle. "Once again, ladies and gentlemen, here's George Benson, from his new album *Breezin'*."

By the time it got to the chorus, the phones had exploded.

After the deejay fielded a few calls, he said, "George, is there anything else on there we can play?"

Right there, right in that studio in New York City, right when jazz fans were digging an album of which I was exceedingly proud, that was one of the most satisfying moments of my professional life. Connecting with an audience at a live show, while not easy, is a smoother process than doing so in a more intimate setting. At a concert, the audience is there to have a good time; the drinks are flowing, and you're holding hands with your sweetheart, so as long as the artists give their all and let their creativity flow, everybody should have a good time. But when something is played on the radio, it might well be doing battle with dinner or housework or a crying baby, so for a song to connect with listeners to the point that they'll drop what they're doing and call up the radio station, well, that means somebody somewhere did something right. When all those kind listeners took the time to give us a ring, I had tangible proof that the record was pretty darn good.

Grinning like a fool, I told the deejay, "I probably already went overboard. I don't know if the folks at the record label would appreciate me giving away all of our secrets so soon."

"I understand, I understand. George, I think I speak for everybody at WRVR when I wish you good luck on what is undoubtedly a special album."

And that good-luck wish worked. After twelve months, the album had sold over four million copies and was nominated for five Grammy Awards, two of which we won: Best Pop Vocal Performance, Male, for "This Masquerade"; and Best Engineered Album, Non-Classical. After that, things started changing. *Drastically.*

The changes were external; me, I was the same guy I'd always been, the guy who showed up to the gig on time, played some music, hung out with the cats, went home, and did it again the next day. But most everybody around me started treating me differently. For instance, folks thought they had all the answers to questions I hadn't even asked, answers they were more than eager to share.

Some cats said stuff like, "Man, it don't matter what the critics say. You keep doing what you're doing. Don't do nothing different. Don't let nobody start telling you what to do."

I'd think, *But* you're *telling me what to do, man,* then say, "I've been making albums for a long time. I think I can take care of it, but thanks."

Other cats told me, "George, you oughta go back to making the kinds of records you made with Brother Jack and Joe Dukes and Lonnie Smith."

I'd think, *People gotta change and grow, man*, then say, "I'm glad you like those other records."

But if I'd learned one thing over the years, it was, if it ain't broke, don't fix it, so the next year, when it came time to plan our next album, we stayed the course: same producer, same engineer, and same musicians, one of whom was our *baaaaad* drummer, Harvey Mason.

I'd known Harvey, who's from Atlantic City, New Jersey, since we were teenagers. I'd seen him go from standout student at the Berklee School of Music in Boston, to the hottest drummer in Hollywood. Whenever we ran into each other, we had a version of the same conversation:

"George, man, I'm gonna make a record with you."

"Okay, brother. We'll make a record."

"I'm serious, George. We're gonna make a record."

"And I'm serious, too, Harvey. We'll make a record."

When Tommy LiPuma suggested during the planning stages of *Breezin'* that we bring Harvey on board, I said, "Yes. Please. Get Harvey Mason if you can." And he was wrong about us making a record together. We made *many* records together, each and every one of which he tore up, and when I say "tore up," I mean tore up with a capital *T*, capital *U*.

In terms of the material, we used the same basic *Breezin'* formula: some jazz stuff, some ballads, some pop stuff, and some vocal stuff. And when it came to the vocal stuff, we stumbled into a good one: "Nature Boy." I'd always loved that gorgeous ballad, especially Nat King Cole's classic version from 1948, so when it was suggested that we give it a shot, I jumped. The question I asked myself was, *Do I try to replicate Nat, or should I pay homage to Nat but also take an entirely different direction?* After much internal discussion, I decided on the latter, and taking that approach was a crucial learning experience. What I learned was that things work out best for me if I stay out of the way of the original. In other words, pay respect to the original version, and then do something else. On "Nature Boy," I changed the tempo and added some of my own vocalese flavor, all while making it obvious that I had much respect—no, *reverence*—for the original. The whole time, I kept it in the back of my head that the listener understood I wasn't trying to be Nat Cole, because there's only one Nat Cole.

I must've done something right, because the song—as well as the album, *In Flight*—was well received in Europe, and in many cases, European jazz fans are considerably tougher than their American counterparts. The French seemed to like the tune even more than everybody else did. During a show in Paris, I finished up "Nature Boy," after which five girls came out of the audience, jumped on the staged, and kissed me, all at the same time. I thought, *What in the world is this? I'm a jazz cat, not one of the Beatles. And I'm thirty-whatever-years-old, and these girls are practically teenagers. Man, I wish this had been going on back in Pittsburgh, or back with Brother Jack.*

Another jazz tune from *In Flight* that seemed to go over quite well was, ironically, written by a cat known first and foremost as a soul singer: Donny Hathaway's "Valdez in the Country." The tune, which Donny had cut three years before for his album *Extension of a Man*—and that's a *baaaaad* album, man, *seriously* bad—was a groovy little thing that gave me a chance to flat-out *play*, without a care in the world. Other musicians must've sensed the fun and freedom that the chord changes, the melody, and the beat allowed for, because over the years it was recorded by about a million other cats; I haven't run the numbers, but I think it was covered more than any other nonstandard tune I've ever recorded. And that pleased me to no end, because Donny was a righteous man.

We spent a fair amount of time together, Donny and I, and to me, he was big-time, so that when we went out on the town, *I* felt big-time. It got to the point where I couldn't relax, I couldn't be myself, because I'd be thinking, *Say, man, I'm hanging with the great Donny Hathaway.* But I was far from the only person who was starstruck in his presence.

One night, after an afternoon of writing songs in his living room, I told him, "We're going uptown," then took him to Minton's Playhouse, figuring it would be a perfect place for him to chill out and hear some music without being accosted for autographs and pictures. Man, was I wrong—when word got out that Donny Hathaway was in the house, pandemonium set in. I was shocked, because I didn't think this hard-core jazz crowd would know Donny from Adam, but his music transcended stylistic boundaries, so everybody knew him—*everybody.* There wasn't a person in that club who wasn't all over that cat.

I wasn't done with Donny's music, not by a long shot. In 2000, I covered his tune "The Ghetto" on my album *Absolute Benson,* and when I do live shows, it's one of my most requested songs. The fact of the matter is, I'll never be done with Donny, because, well, here's a confession: I tried to steal his vocal technique. His voice had so much air in it, soft and yet powerful at the same time, and his phrasing was out of this world. Everything that came out of his throat was soulful, heartfelt, and honest. Add in his experience with gospel music, and he was unbeatable. Donny passed away in 1979, and I never found the right moment to express to him his crucial role in my musical evolution. I always wondered how he would've felt had he known.

In Flight didn't go over the moon like *Breezin',* but it made its fair share of noise and landed me a platinum record, as well as a connection that would change the course of my career . . . and, for that matter, my entire life.

In 1977, unless you were a *serious* Diana Ross fan, you probably didn't know the name Michael Masser, but chances are you knew his music, because at that point, he'd written or cowritten some of Ross the Boss's best-selling songs of the 1970s, including "Touch Me in the Morning," "Last Time I Saw Him," "Together," "Sorry Doesn't Make It Right," and, most notably, "Do You Know Where You're Going To." I certainly knew those songs, but I had no idea who the composer was, so when somebody said that Michael was trying to track me down, I didn't think anything of it.

That summer, I was invited to an industry party in Beverly Hills, a party filled with VIPs and record bigwigs as far as the eye could see. It was, without question, the most opulent, over-the-top event I'd ever attended. The big room was beautiful, the decorations were beautiful, the high-end food was beautiful, and heck, even the chairs were beautiful.

Another thing about those chairs: They made for good weapons. And I know that because one of the partygoers picked up one of those beautiful chairs and whupped another partygoer in the head, which led to a fight. Now I'd been in my fair share of fights, and this one was pretty weak—we're talking about a roomful of record executives who'd probably never raised a fist in their lives. There was a lot of pushing, shoving, and food throwing, and to the untrained eye—and the party was full of untrained eyes—it must've looked like a riot.

Me, I stayed seated at the table and finished my dinner.

As I was calmly dabbing the corner of my mouth with a napkin, I noticed a guy on the floor, on all fours, navigating his way in between splayed legs and fallen bodies. I tapped my wife, Johnnie, on the shoulder and said, "Honey, there's a crazy Caucasian cat crawling on the floor in our direction. If he comes over here and says anything, don't pay him no mind. Because I darn sure won't."

Sure enough, he came to our table, pulled himself up into a chair, and started talking. I ignored him and dived into my dessert; he was completely unfazed and kept right on talking. All I heard out of him was, "Blah, blah, blah, blah, blah, Muhammad Ali."

That perked my ears up. I loved the Greatest of All Time—heck, anybody with a heart, a soul, and the love of a good rope-a-dope loved the Greatest of All Time. I dropped my fork and said, "Muhammad Ali? What do you know about Ali?"

He said, "I'm doing the music to his film. And I have a tune for you to sing."

"What film?" I asked.

"These two guys, Tom Gries and Monte Hellman, are making a movie about Ali called *The Greatest*. Ali's playing himself. It's gonna be huge."

Hmm, I thought, *it's interesting that a Caucasian guy is writing the music for a film about the most popular, best-known African American in the world.* But I thought about it for a second more, and it dawned on me that Muhammad Ali wasn't just the best-known African American in the world—he was darn near the best-known *person* in the world, regardless of color, race, or creed. That being the case, it didn't matter whether the guy who composed the sound track was black, white, brown, or yellow.

And then I remembered a famous quote from Miles Davis. This was in the early 1970s, when he had Chick Corea and Keith Jarrett playing keyboards in his band, and somebody asked him why he'd hired so many white guys. His answer: "I don't care if a dude is purple with green breath, as long as he can swing."

Which begged the question, could this dude swing?

I asked, "What kind of stuff have you done?"

"Well, I wrote 'Touch Me in the Morning.'"

"You mean that Diana Ross song?"

"Yeah," he said.

"That's a *baaaaad* tune, man," I said.

"I also wrote 'Theme from *Mahogany*.' You know, 'Do You Know Where You're Going To.'"

I said, "You did? You wrote that? That's awesome, man. What'd you say your name is again?"

"I didn't say. It's Michael Masser."

"Oh, *you're* Michael Masser. Heard you've been looking for me."

I think he could tell that he didn't have my attention before, but he had it now, so he repeated, "Yeah, like I was saying, I've got this song I wrote for Muhammad's film, and I'd like you to do it."

"Man, if you wrote 'Do You Know Where You're Going To,' I'm interested. Give me your number."

The following week, I took a ride up to his house in the Hollywood Hills. The second I got in the door, he dragged me over to the piano and started in on a beautiful melody, then burst out singing:

> *I believe that children are our future*
> *Teach them well and let them lead the way*
> *Show them all the beauty they possess inside*
> *Give them a sense of pride to make it easier.*

The rest of the tune was equally positive, uplifting, and lovely, and I fell in love with it instantly. After the final note was finished ringing, I said, "I'm in. What's it called?"

"'The Greatest Love of All.' But there's a problem. A big problem."

Of course there is, I thought. *It's the record industry. There's always a problem.* "And that problem is . . . ?"

Michael said, "The problem is, Arista Records owns the sound track."

"Ah. You're right. That is a problem." Record labels were (and still are) proprietary about their artists. From Arista's perspective, since they were the ones putting out the sound track, they'd want somebody on their roster to do the song, because if it hit hard, a buyer might want to check out something from the singer's back catalog, thus ensuring Arista a few more sales. Warner Bros., on the other hand, didn't want one of its artists helping make money for the competition. It was a conundrum.

"But I don't care about Arista," Michael said. "I still want you to do it."

"I'm flattered, man," I said, "and I love that tune, and I know I'd sing the heck out of it. But why make trouble for yourself? Arista's got some good people in their stable. Use one of them."

He said, "You're the guy, George. I want you because you sound like Muhammad. You've both got that fogginess in your voices. I bet you could do a mean Ali impression."

It just so happened that I *did* do a mean Ali impression, so I launched into it: "Clay comes out to meet Liston and Liston starts to retreat / If Liston goes back an inch farther he'll end up in a ringside seat / Clay swings with his left, Clay swings with his right / Look at young Cassius carry the fight / Liston keeps backing, but there's not enough room / It's a matter of time till Clay lowers the boom."

Michael busted out laughing. "That, George Benson, is why you need to do this song. So let's make it happen."

Sure enough, Warner Bros. wanted me to have nothing to do with the tune—it turned out that Warner Bros. and Arista were archenemies. (I found out later that during that hypercompetitive era, most every label hated most every other label with a passion.) But somebody convinced somebody somewhere that it would benefit everybody if I were allowed to cut this track, so the proper papers were signed, and off I went to record a song that practically launched me into the next phase of my life.

When the record came out—and the turnaround time in those days was fast; it seemed like it was in stores only a couple weeks after the session—it got airplay everywhere at the same time: jazz radio, pop radio, R&B radio, adult contemporary, *everywhere*. Thanks to its visibility, I received twice as many concert offers, and the promoters were paying me twice as much as I'd earned just a few months before.

(I sang another one of Michael's tunes on the sound track of *The Greatest*, called "I Always Knew I Had It in Me." I thought it was a better tune, but lyrically speaking, the public apparently felt it didn't have as much depth, so it didn't connect with an audience on the same level. But it was a killer.)

Late one night (or early one morning) of the week that "The Greatest Love of All" snuck into the *Billboard* Top 40, the phone rang. After I mumbled hello, somebody said, "Hey, George."

Immediately, I knew that voice. It was a voice I'd heard on television and on the radio hundreds of times. It was the voice that had taunted Sonny Liston, insulted Joe Frazier, teased George Foreman, and told the government, "I ain't got no quarrel with no Viet Cong."

"Muhammad!" I said, suddenly wide awake.

"George, I just heard that record of yours. I want you to tell me one thing."

"What's that?" I asked.

"Were you thinking about me when you cut that?"

When I was in the studio, I concentrated on the music. I didn't think about anything or anybody other than what I needed to do in the moment. But I loved Ali, so I told him, "You know what I was thinking about? I was thinking about being *baaaaad*, man, because, champ, you're a *baaaaad, baaaaad* man."

He laughed and said, "That's all I wanted to know, baby. That's all I wanted to know. It's a great record, George. You made me proud." And then he hung up.

So "The Greatest Love of All" was big, but there was one more game-changer to come.

Since my days with the Altairs, I'd undergone multiple musical metamorphoses: from blues cat to blues-jazz cat . . . from blues-jazz cat to jazz cat . . . from jazz cat to soul-jazz cat . . . and from soul-jazz cat to R&B-jazz cat. But throughout all those phases—some of which were pretty radical—I never lost my love for doo-wop.

Doo-wop had been out of vogue since the mid-1960s—the Altairs caught the tail end of that wave, thank goodness—but many of those compositions continued to sound fresh and relevant, one of which was "On Broadway," by the Drifters. The tune, which was a modest hit for them in 1963, was about the dashing of big-city dreams, about trying to make it as a performer in a world that doesn't always support artists, about fighting the odds, no matter how high against you the deck is stacked—these themes are timeless and were as meaningful in 1979 as they were in 1969, and would be in 1999. Also, it was funky as all get-out, plus it featured trumpeters Joe Newman and Ernie Royal from Count Basie's band, as well as my main man Billy Butler on guitar. I was a veritable doo-wop historian, and at any given moment, I had one of thousands of doo-wop tunes running through my head, but "On Broadway" stood out. So in the middle of 1977, when we were picking out material for a live album we were going to record that fall at the Roxy Theatre in West Hollywood, I threw it out there, and it stuck.

As was the case with "Nature Boy," we made the song our own. While paying implied homage to the Drifters, nobody could say we copied the original, but nobody could say we ignored it. When it came time to cut the album—a record that would come to be called *Weekend in L.A.*—the song hadn't been road-tested. We hadn't played it a thousand times at a thousand shows, so we didn't have it *down*. Sometimes it takes years of performing a song to get it just right, and that even goes for an original composition. Just because you wrote it doesn't mean you know it . . . *yet*. The only way to get inside of a song is to experiment, but experimentation isn't done when you're surrounded by tens of thousands of dollars of recording equipment and highly paid engineers . . . unless you're a daredevil like me.

During the first set of the first show at the Roxy, I hadn't yet figured out the tune's tempo. The Drifters took it at a slow, finger-snapping tempo, so I counted it off with that in mind. That loping groove was perfect for a doo-wop tune but too slow for a jazz tune, so in the second set, I adjusted the tempo. The problem was, I adjusted it about twenty-four bars into the tune, right before I sang the first line: "They say the neon lights are bright, on Brrrooooooooooadwayyyyyy." But the band caught on quick—little wonder; it was the same batch of cats from *Breezin'* and *In Flight*, and we'd developed the level of communication you can only achieve after playing hours, days, weeks, months, and years of music together—and the crowd started clapping, and that spurred me on, big-time. I could tell by the smiling faces both in front of the stage and on the stage that something special was happening. By the time it got to my solo, chills ran down my spine, into my feet, then back up to my hands.

I was so wrapped up in the moment that I didn't realize we played for over ten minutes.

That may not seem like an issue, but let me give you some perspective: In 1978, the average single you heard on your average AM radio station was in the three-minute range. The folks on the FM side of the dial had loosened things up, and they'd play album cuts that went on as long as seven or eight minutes. Unless a renegade deejay had an insatiable urge to play John Coltrane's *A Love Supreme* in its entirety, jazz stations usually capped out at ten minutes. Most of the radio formats on which I was played—soul, pop, R&B, and adult contemporary—wouldn't even consider having anything to do with a fourteen-minute cut. What listener would stay tuned for that long? What advertiser would tolerate its ad being bumped for a tune that had a three-minute percussion jam? That song was dead in the water before it even had a chance to get wet.

Tommy LiPuma didn't care. After the show, he said, "That's good enough for me." But I wouldn't be sure if it was good enough for *me* until I heard it on tape. We asked the engineer to dub us a cassette so we could go back to the hotel and check it out. So we checked it out. Then we checked it out again. Then again. And again. And again and again and again. We listened to that song for hours, thrilled with the performance but doubly thrilled with the audience response. See, we'd never gotten a response like that before, and we'd gotten plenty of good responses over the previous fifteen years, so that's saying something. I believed we had ourselves a hit on our hands.

The afternoon before the next night's show, Tommy and I were hanging out at his house, listening to some of the previous evening's material, and he put on the first version of "On Broadway," the one that was *way* too slow. I made a nasty face and said, "Tommy, take that off, man. That's not the one."

He said, "George, this sounds fantastic. I'm telling you, this is . . ."

I cut him off. "Tommy, last night we played a version of this song that I know in my heart is going to be a smash. The crowd was into it, the cats were into it, and I was into it, and I know that the people who buy this record are gonna be into it."

Shaking his head, Tommy said, "I didn't hear that, George. I didn't hear anything like that last night at all." He paused, then added, "Besides, I think we erased it."

I can only imagine the expression on my face. Maintaining my cool, I asked, "What did you say?"

"Yeah, we're running out of tape, so we went over it."

I stared at Tommy for a good minute, then stomped out the front door, jumped into my rental car, and drove back to the hotel at about a thousand miles per hour, darn near as mad as I'd ever been. See, when it comes to an improvisation-based art like jazz, it's essential that when you're cutting an album, either live or in the studio, if a moment with a capital *M* is captured on tape, you hold onto it for dear life. Sure, it's possible that the magic can be recaptured, and even improved upon, but you don't know that. Even if the circumstances are exactly the same—same musicians, same equalization, same temperature, same clothes, same lunch—there's no guarantee you'll have the same vibe. Vibes are elusive, man.

I took a long, hot shower in order to cool down my steaming head; while I was drying off, the phone rang: Tommy LiPuma. "Yeah?" I grunted.

"George, I think we found the tape."

"You *think*? You're not *sure*?"

"We're *pretty* sure. Come back to the house and we'll suss it out."

I got dressed and sped over to Tommy's pad, hoping against hope that he was right, that he'd tracked down the *right* version, the *beautiful* version, the *magical* version. When I arrived, I parked myself on his sofa and said, "Let's hear this hit now, man. Put the hit on."

He said, "Okay, but I still think the first one sounded good."

"Too slow, man. Put on the hit."

Tommy repeated, "The first one sounded good."

Then I repeated, "Put on the hit, Tommy."

He sighed, then hit Play on the cassette recorder, and, man, that thing was rocking from bar one. Tommy's head was perceptibly bobbing.

"I see you moving, man," I said. "That's a hit record. If I ever heard one, that's a hit record."

We listened three more times, and finally, he said, "All right, George. I agree with you. You're right. It's a hit."

Tommy and I work well together—hand in glove, even—but we have one key philosophical disagreement: He's about the music, and I'm about the audience. I know that when he listened to the longer, *proper* version of "On Broadway," the things that grabbed him were (a) the length, which I'm certain he felt would keep us from reaching a wide audience, and (b) the fact that the tempo wasn't locked in from the start. I suspect that he was looking for a six-minute version of the song that sounded like it was cut to a click track, and there's nothing wrong with that . . . when you're in the studio. But when you're recording something live, you want it to sound live, warts and all.

Where Tommy is a perfection guy, I'm a crowd guy. See, I've been looking into the faces of audience members ever since I was a kid, and when I go somewhere to perform, I'm there for one reason: to make people glad they came. And on that tape—what with all the clappin', cheerin', whoopin', and hollerin'—it was obvious to anybody with a working set of ears that the paying customers were glad to be there. We captured it, and—thank goodness—we were able to keep it.

Tommy tried to convince us that we should chop a minute or three from the song, in order to get more airplay. I understood that, but I couldn't bring myself to pull out the machete. What was I going to cut out? The intro where the crowd is shouting "Wooooo," even though they don't know the song? The guitar solo? (You can't edit a solo and make it sound good unless you're Miles Davis and the album is *Bitches Brew*). The percussion jam that sent the crowd over the moon? No, that long version of "On Broadway" was *the* version of "On

Broadway," forever and ever until the end of time. Admittedly, if we'd chopped it in half, more folks would've heard it on the radio— and several years later, an edited version was released, which did make it onto the air on a regular basis—but that long one, well, man, it *worked*, to the tune of a platinum record and a couple weeks perched atop the *Billboard* R&B chart. But one aspect of which I'm most proud is the fact that thanks in part to *Weekend in L.A.*, "On Broadway" went from being a semi-obscure doo-wop tune to a modern jazz and pop standard, covered by everybody from Tito Puente to Neil Young to James Taylor.

So *Weekend* did well, but I had no time to rest on my laurels, such as they were. In that era, you weren't allowed to release an album, then tour off of it for two years. You had to fire off record after record after record, *bam, bam, bam*, and anybody who tells you that's an easy thing is lying through their teeth. Let me amend that: Yes, you can fire off record after record after record, but if the records aren't good, the quantity isn't going to make up for a lack of quality. That all being the case, I knew that my album for 1979 would require some sort of change, and that change came in the form of a cat whom I consider to be one of the greatest guitarists in all of the world.

Back in my CTI days, my band regularly played a club in Detroit called Baker's Keyboard Lounge. Now, Baker's wasn't as well known as the Village Vanguard or Minton's Playhouse or the Jazz Workshop or the London House or the Jazz Showcase or the Green Mill—or any of those other joints in New York, California, or Chicago—but it should've been, because Baker's was founded in 1934 (Can you dig that? 1934, man! It opened when Franklin Roosevelt was president; from FDR to Obama and beyond), and that stage has hosted everybody from Pops to Nat Cole to Ella to Miles to Trane, so you know there's some fairy dust up there.

Baker's is right off of Eight Mile Road, which isn't the greatest neighborhood in the world—never has been, probably never will be— so it was rare to see any young cats out there; after all, if I'd lived in

Detroit, I wouldn't let my teenagers near the place. Besides, since it was such a dicey area, there was a noticeable police presence, and the club owners, not wanting to attract trouble, never admitted under-age kids—that is, most of the time.

The club was founded by Clarence Baker, but in 1963, he leased it to a cat named Solly Hartstein. Solly was also an artist manager, and one of his clients was a young guitarist—and when I say "young," I mean *prodigy* young—named Earl Klugh. Earl wasn't legally allowed into Baker's, so in order to help the kid get a jazz education, Solly would sneak him into the club and sit him in a dark corner so he could check out the acts that came through, acts like Oscar Peterson, Sonny Stitt, and George Shearing, as well as local cats like Donald Byrd, Tommy Flanagan, and Barry Harris.

Word was he also dug a guitarist by the name of George Benson.

One night after a gig, Solly pulled me aside and said, "George, I'd like you to listen to this boy, Earl. I think he's a great player, but I'd like to get your opinion."

I said, "We're rehearsing here at the club tomorrow afternoon." When my band was on the road, we rehearsed every day—after all, we had nothing else to do. "Bring him on down."

The next afternoon, after we finished up running down our set list and experimenting with a few new ideas, I invited Earl onto the bandstand. He ambled over—and I truly mean ambled; Earl is a slow mover—then he unpacked his acoustic guitar, sat down on a stool, and fumbled around for a while, jiggling this and tuning that. Finally I grew impatient and snapped, "Come on, man!" I probably sounded harsher than necessary.

Politely, Earl said, "Sorry, sorry, sorry," then started playing, and, man, I heard real talent. He had perfect technique and a perfect finger style, all without a pick. After he finished up his tune, I asked, "Where'd you learn how to play like that?" What he was doing, you couldn't pick up on your own.

He said, "I studied with a man who studied with Andrés Segovia."

I said, "I can hear it—and see it—because your technique is perfect. You make no mistakes."

Earl flashed a shy, sheepish grin, then said, "Thanks, George. I can also play with a pick, but I don't like to."

I said, "Man, don't play with a pick. You're perfect the way you are."

That night, Solly all but ran over and asked, "How do you like him? He's a *baaaaad* little guy, right?"

I said, "I think he's fantastic."

"Good," Solly said. "So do something for this kid. Take him out on the road or something."

This was way before *Breezin'* came out, so I had little to no juice in the music industry. "Solly, I can't do nothing for myself, let alone something for somebody else."

"Okay, but do me a favor and keep him in the back of your head."

I thought of all the cats who'd helped me along the way, and said, "I will, man. I promise." And I did.

A few weeks later, when I was getting ready to go into the studio to record the album *White Rabbit*, I called Earl. "Earl, how'd you like to make a record with me?"

He said, "Yeah, man, yeah." Earl was quiet, but I could tell he was thrilled, and knowing he was thrilled, thrilled me.

When I brought him to New York, we rehearsed a composition of mine called "El Mar," a relatively complex tune with what I hoped was a hip Latin feel. Earl reads music as well as anybody I've ever worked with, so when I put the chart on his music stand, he didn't blink. When the red light went on, he crushed it.

After the session, I asked Creed Taylor, "Man, how do you like this kid?"

Creed shrugged. "He's all right." I suspect that Creed was less apt to get excited about somebody unless he'd discovered him.

"I was going to ask you to give him a deal," I said, "but if you think he's just *all right*, then I don't want you to sign him. If you don't love him, don't bother. I don't want him to sit in no record company on the back burners."

Earl had been on the road with my band for almost a year when he got a call from George Shearing, who offered him a spot in his trio. The venerable blind pianist was one of the more popular cats on the scene, so he worked all the time. Earl told me about Shearing, then said, "I don't know if I want to take it."

I said, "Earl, man, are you crazy? You gotta take that gig, because you'll get to play every night with a cat who uses harmonies you've never even tried. Plus, he's experienced and a true professional, and that'll rub off on you. It'll make you a better player and a better person."

So he went on the road with Shearing, and sure enough, his playing jumped up a few notches, and he developed confidence—and deservedly so—to the point that he believed he was ready for his own record deal. So I invited him to my studio in my garage in the Bronx and said, "Brother, let's make you a demo tape." We laid down four tracks, which I mixed down and sent to a handful of music industry heavies, one of whom was George Butler, a producer and A&R man who was working for Solid State Records, which, at the time, was overseeing Blue Note.

A couple weeks later, Butler rang me up. "George, I got that tape you sent me, that thing by Earl Klugh . . ." (He pronounced "Klugh" like "glug"; the proper pronounciation is "clue." I set him straight.) "Is it true he's only nineteen years old? That can't be right. Because what I'm hearing on that tape could not have come from a nineteen-year-old."

"He's nineteen," I said. "And it came from him. I was there."

Sounding unconvinced, Butler continued, "And he's playing classical guitar, and he says he's black."

"Yeah, that's right. He's African American."

He says, "I don't believe it."

"You don't believe it? You want to see it with your own eyes? Then send him a plane ticket, man." So he flew Earl out to New York, and next thing you know, he has a record for which yours truly was fortunate enough to write the liner notes.

Earl's self-titled debut came out just a little after *Breezin'*, and that record was badder than bad; for that matter, I firmly believe that if it weren't for *Breezin'*, Earl would've been the biggest thing in jazz. The record sold over 300,000 copies, and if *Breezin'* hadn't gone crazy, he would've been the toast of the town. (When word got out about how many copies Earl moved, I could see Creed Taylor thumping his head against the wall over and over again, livid that he hadn't listened to me.)

Since then, Earl had cut a couple of other albums that were equally successful, and his playing was better than ever, so I decided to bring him on board for my next album, *Livin' Inside Your Love*, knowing that his gorgeous acoustic guitar sound would give us another layer of color. I was so thrilled with what he was doing that I couldn't stop writing or picking new material. By the time it was all said and done, we had twelve songs in the can, all of which most everybody at the label seemed to dig, so we had to put it out as a double album. Now, a double album wasn't double the cost of a single album, but it was nonetheless pricier, so it didn't sell as well as the previous three Warner Bros. titles. (*Weekend in L.A.* was also a double record set, but it featured "On Broadway," which made it an album of destiny.) The label didn't put a lot of pressure on me to come up with something chartworthy, but they didn't *not* put a lot of pressure on me, if you know what I mean. So I decided to call in one of the heaviest of the heavy.

Quincy Jones is one of the most revered figures in music history, but I don't think he gets *enough* credit. Your typical cat on the street thinks of Q first and foremost as a producer—the guy who helped turn Michael Jackson into a megastar, the guy who's been called upon by everybody from Frank Sinatra to Aretha Franklin to Lena Horne, an ageless wonder who transcends eras and styles so much so that contemporary rappers like Jay-Z and Kanye West broke the bank to pay for his services. But what the typical cat on the street has forgotten (or didn't know in the first place) is what Q has done for jazz. They might not know that he was a phenomenal trumpeter, and played in the big bands of Dizzy Gillespie and Lionel Hampton before he even turned thirty. They might not know that he arranged original compositions for Duke Ellington, Count Basie, Gene Krupa, Cannonball Adderley, Tommy Dorsey, Dinah Washington, and Sarah Vaughan. They might not know that on the album *Genius + Soul = Jazz*, he practically turned Ray Charles into a full-time jazz cat. Simply put, Quincy Jones is the Man.

Back in the day, Q and I didn't run in the same circles, but because we're both obsessive workers who're almost always out on the road doing *something*, our paths had crossed many times, and we'd spent a bit of time in the studio together. For instance, one summer 1975 evening in Chicago, we ran into each other at a party at the John Hancock building. I said to him, "Man, we need to work together. I'm looking forward to finally doing something with you."

Nodding, Q said, "I got a thing coming up in L.A. We're having a battle of the big bands. I'm putting together a group with Jimmy Smith and a few other cats. You play alongside organists as well as anybody. Why don't you come aboard?" So I did, and it was a blast. We vowed that someday we'd do a record. But *Breezin'* came out and went to the moon, and Q was producing massive hit records for Michael Jackson and the Brothers Johnson, so we did our own things and kept in touch. At some point during our periodic chats, one of us would inevitably repeat, "Man, we gotta do a record together."

In 1980, Warner Bros. and Quincy partnered on a subsidiary label called Qwest, which gave Quincy the chance to make whatever records he wanted to make . . . and, much to my luck, he still wanted to make a George Benson record. So the proper meetings were held, and the proper papers were signed, and, next thing you know, I'm the first cat on Quincy's label.

When it got time to plan the record, I went to Q's crib, where he sat me down, looked me right in the eye, and said, "George, I got a question for you."

"Okay," I said, inwardly smiling at his seriousness and intensity.

"Do you want to make the greatest jazz record in the history of the world?"

Laughing, I said, "The greatest jazz record has already been made, Q. Charlie Parker put that stuff to bed years ago with 'Just Friends,' on *Charlie Parker with Strings*. I can't compete with that stuff. *Nobody* can."

He nodded. "Fair enough. Then let me ask you this: Do you want to go for the throat?"

"Quincy," I said, "let's go for the throat, baby. Let's go for the throat."

For Q, going for the throat meant putting together a collection of musicians that was second to none, a true A-team. It seemed like he called up every keyboardist in his phone book: Herbie Hancock, George Duke, Richard Tee, Clare Fischer, Mike Boddicker, and a young cat named Gregory Phillinganes. Greg was Earl Klugh's childhood pal from Detroit; he'd sat in with me one night at Baker's Keyboard Lounge, and I knew he'd be something special. (And I was right—he *was* special, so special that for the next two-plus decades, we recorded and toured together at every given opportunity, which is more times than I can count.)

When we started discussing percussionists, I said, "Man, if we're putting together an all-star team, I need the greatest drummer you have."

Without hesitation, he said, "J.R."

"J.R.?" I said.

"Yeah. John Robinson. I used him on *Off the Wall*."

Now, when people listen to Michael Jackson records, they usually don't focus in on the drummer, but what John Robinson was doing on *Off the Wall* was perfection with soul. He sounded like the funkiest drum machine you'd ever want to hear. "Don't leave him out! He's A-team! He's an all-star!"

Once we were happy with our sidemen game plan, we went on to discuss material. (That was one of the best parts of working with Qwest: Quincy was in charge of *everything*, which meant we didn't have to talk with *this* person to approve *that* budget, and *that* person to approve *this* song. Q was A&R man, accountant, and producer, all wrapped up into one. Talk about a time saver.) I told him, "Lately, I've been digging on Latin-based things."

Q scratched his chin. "Interesting. Any reason in particular?"

"Yeah. Because the rhythm is so solid, I can slide in between the notes and beats, do my thing, and end up exactly where I need to be."

"I think I know what you're talking about." He stood up and motioned me over to his insanely big record library. "I've got some stuff for you to check out."

First he played me a series of African records, most of which were *baaaaad*, but none of which grabbed me. Then he played me some salsa, samba, and rumba stuff, and again, while it was quality material, it wasn't the music I'd been hearing in my head. Finally he put on something by a cat from Rio de Janeiro named Ivan Lins. I wasn't hip to Ivan, but I darn sure should've been, because he'd been making unbelievable Brazilian-based jazz and pop since the early 1970s. The first thing he played me was a gorgeous ballad called "Love Dance." It was quiet but intense, slow but potent, beautiful yet heartbreaking. I said, "What in the world is that? That's *mean*."

"You dig that?" Q said. "Then check this out."

Next up was "Dinorah, Dinorah," which had that combination of Latin and soul for which I'd been seeking. "Man, *that's* the stuff I'm talking about!" I almost ran across the room and gave Quincy a bear hug.

"So you want to do these? Does this satisfy your Latin craving?"

"Yes and yes!" I said.

"Cool," he said, grabbing his phone book. "Let me make a quick call." He dialed, then, after a minute or three, said, "Hello? . . . Ivan? . . . Can you hear me? . . . It's Q . . . Listen, my Brazilian brother from another mother, I'm sitting here in my house with George Benson . . . That's right, George Benson the guitarist, and he *loves* your music . . . Yeah, he wants to put a couple of your songs on his next record . . . We're doing it for my label . . . Yeah, it *is* cool. So do you want to come up and help out? . . . Um, sure, tomorrow's fine . . . Yeah, I'll cover your flight . . . Cool, see you then, baby." And that's Quincy Jones in a nutshell: You bring him an idea, you kick it around, he comes up with some suggestions that make it better than you could've imagined, then he flies over some cat on the other side of the world to help bring it to life. And it's a good thing Ivan joined us, because he approaches harmony in a manner that was *way* above and beyond anything I'd ever learned. (He even taught Quincy a thing or two.) He straightened us out on some stuff, stuff that made those two tunes something special.

As I mentioned, Q and I are *workers*, and when we get going, there's no stopping us. Once we started recording, we were in the studio for a month—all day, all night, every day—tracking, experimenting, tweaking. Quincy is a one-of-a-kind collaborator, willing to listen to any idea or try anything, unconcerned if his own ideas don't work. His only goal is to make the best record possible; it doesn't matter if the best concept comes from him or me or some cat he ran into on his way to the soda machine.

Sometimes his ideas seemed straight-up radical. One morning a couple of weeks into the session, he pulled me aside and said, "You know that tune we put in the can yesterday?"

"In the can" meant that it was done. "Yeah," I said. " 'Love X Love.' "

"Yeah, well, Rod wrote some lyrics for the tune. He'd like to try them out."

Rod was Rod Temperton, an unbelievably talented composer and arranger from the U.K. He'd done work with Quincy since the mid-1970s, but their partnership was sealed forever and ever on *Off the Wall,* on which he wrote the title cut, "Burn This Disco Out," and, in a move that gave him musical immortality, "Rock with You." Rod was *baaaaad,* no question about it. But . . .

"Man, I dig it as an instrumental," I said. Besides, something I'd learned about Rod in the brief time we'd been working together: He was never satisfied with his lyrics. He'd hand you one set of words, you'd cut it, and you'd be happy; then he'd show up to the studio the next day with ten different new sets of lyrics. Whenever it happened—and it happened more times than I'd care to discuss—I'd pull Quincy aside and say, "You guys gotta pick something, man. If it keeps up like this, it'll never end."

As usual, Q would keep his cool. "Don't worry about it, George. We're gonna get it."

I'd think, *This cat's signing the checks, so I guess his word is law.* But it turned out that he and Rod were right to take their time, to add lyrics, to change things up even when it seemed like we were good to go. And I'm not just talking about "Love X Love"—I'm talking about the entire album.

The tune that I expected to be that album's "This Masquerade" was called "One Hundred Ways," a pretty little mid-tempo ballad that I envisioned would have an entire audience snapping their fingers in unison. The afternoon after we finished it up, Quincy told me, "George, the Warner Bros. people are having a party tonight, and they want to hear what the artists are doing. So I told them I'd be over with one of your cuts."

"Cool. What're you gonna play them?"

"I'm taking 'One Hundred Ways.'"

"I agree with that one hundred percent."

According to Q, "One Hundred Ways" blew the party away, but once they put on a new thing by Larry Graham called "One in a Million," people kind of forgot about "One Hundred Ways," so we ended up leaving it off of the record. (If you want to hear the tune, check out Q's album *The Dude*. That version is something else, man; James Ingram sang the heck out of it.)

It turned out Q and Rod made the right choices—the tunes and their respective lyrics were on point—so we put the album to bed, thrilled to pieces at the result. It was the most intense, concentrated work I've ever done in the studio—long nights of take after take after take—and even though I was satisfied with the result, I couldn't wait for a day or two away from the studio.

Unfortunately, the next day: *Brrrrrrring*. "Hello?"

"George, it's Quincy. We have one more tune to record."

"*What?* Man, my mind is already on vacation. So's my voice. And my fingers."

"One more tune, baby. You can do it!"

"No, Q, come on. I'm wiped. I've got nothing left. I couldn't sing a lick."

Quincy wouldn't let up. "I'm telling you, man, Rod wrote this one just for you, and it's *baaaaad*. We just want to try it out and see if it means anything."

I knew this would go on all day and all night, so I said, "All right, fine. What time do you want me?"

"Ten minutes ago. We got all the tracks done, everything: bass, drums, horns, keys, rhythm guitars, everything. All you have to do is lay down your guitar part, sing the song, and it'll be done. You'll be in and out of here in two hours. And I brought in Lee Ritenour; maybe he'll make your life easier." Lee was one of the badder young guitarists on the scene. He was a go-to studio cat but had put out a few terrific solo albums—my favorite was called *Captain Fingers*. The guy could play.

When I arrived at the studio, Quincy didn't waste any time. After he dialed me in—which took no time, because Q knew how to make my guitar sound exactly how it should sound—he said, "First of all, it needs some guitar licks. Play that squiggly thing." Q had developed a list of silly names for my various formulas, so I knew exactly what "squiggly" meant. So I played the squiggly thing, after which he told Lee, "Try playing it in unison with him, baby."

I then told Lee, "Yeah, you play the upper part, and I'll play it lower." And darned if it didn't sound pretty good. I was getting into it. I was glad Quincy made me come down.

Until it got time to sing.

Man, Rod Temperton was all over me about the vocals: "George, you don't have the vibe . . . George, sing my melody . . . George, you don't have the vibe . . . George, try it again . . . George, you don't have the vibe . . . George, don't sing your melody . . . George, you don't have the vibe . . . George, do it as written . . . George, you don't have the vibe . . ." Fed up, I finally got *strict* with the song. I sang it exactly the way Rod conveyed he wanted it sung, and I mean *exactly.*

When we finished up that take, Rod sighed and said, "George, can you loosen up a bit?"

Aaaaaaaaaargh!

After another 5,157 takes—okay, maybe it was ten or fifteen, but it felt like 5,157—I said, "Q, man, I'm tired. That's it."

"Okay. I think we've got it. I think out of all those tracks, we can piece it together." He paused, gave me a speculative look, then said, "But before you go home, can you try it like this?" And then he sang the beginning of the first verse in a raspy voice:

> *Whenever dark has fallen*
> *You know the spirit of the party starts to come alive*
> *Until the day is dawning*
> *You can throw out all the blues and hit the city lights*

I said, "What do you mean, do one like that?"

He said, "Do one with that voice."

"Man, no. You might put that out on a record. I can't be all rasping for the world to hear."

Quincy said, "No, no, no, no, no, I'm not gonna put it on anything. I just want to see what it sounds like."

Sighing, I said, "If I do it like that, you promise you'll let me go?"

"I promise."

"And only one take, right?"

"Only one take."

"Fine. Let's do it."

And I did it with the rasp in just one take. And that became the title cut of the album *Give Me the Night.* And that's why Quincy Jones is Quincy Jones. He heard something in his head that I never, ever, ever would've considered. Who would think, *Man, if I beat and batter my voice for an entire day, it'll sound great on this tune.* Quincy Jones, that's who.

Heeding my stepfather's advice, I knew I needed to put a straight-up jazz song on the album, so I told Q that I wanted to take a crack at "Moody's Mood for Love." When it was first recorded in 1949, "Moody's Mood" was tenor saxophonist James Moody's take on the old standard "I'm in the Mood for Love." (Moody, by the way, is one of the most unsung of the unsung. He wasn't an early bebop innovator like Bird, Diz, or Miles, but he was right there alongside of them, playing his backside off, adding his own slick, thick twist to the burgeoning style.) Three years later, Eddie Jefferson put words to Moody's solo, which wasn't easy, because that solo was dense, man—full of double-time runs, huge intervallic leaps, and odd rhythms. But Eddie's brain didn't work like everybody else's, so he came up with a hip little first-person narrative about a cat singing a love song to his girl; in it, he spends a lot of time discussing the weather: hurricanes, rain, clouds, and the like. It's funny, swinging, and smart, so little wonder that most every jazz vocalist likes to take a crack at it.

I tried recording it back when I was with CTI. Creed Taylor, who apparently didn't care for vocalese—that's what it's called when a cat writes lyrics to the melody of an improvised solo, *vocalese*—thought it was a bad idea and tried to talk me out of it, but before he could get too far, I said, "Man, put a microphone on me. Let's do this." So he did, and in the middle of the take, the guys in the band started booing. And it wasn't just "Boo, boo," it was "Booooooooooooo! *Booooooo!* BOOOOOOOOOO!"

To his credit, Creed didn't give me an "I told you so." He calmly said, "We'll do one full take, then we'll move on."

A couple of years later, due to a timing and contract quirk, I had to cut a record for CTI after *Breezin'* was already in the can. There was a buzz about my vocals, so Creed asked me if I wanted to do some vocalese for the album that would come to be called *Good King Bad.* I glared at him and said, "Creed, you don't like those things! Remember? So don't ask me to do something that I already know you don't like." (It turned out that he fooled me: In 1983, a good three years after my Qwest version of "Moody's Mood" made some noise, Creed released the inferior CTI version on a collection of unissued tracks. He never got my approval.)

I was beyond pleased with *Give Me the Night,* because more than any album to that point, it demonstrated all of my musical loves: R&B, soul, Latin, and bebop. It wasn't a contrived effort to please everybody, or to sell records, but an extension of me—an attempt to share everything inside my heart, my head, and my ears. For weeks after we were done with the final mix, I drove around Beverly Hills at night in my rented car and listened to that tape over and over again. (Part of the magic came courtesy of Bruce Swedien, one of the greatest sound engineers on this planet. I don't know how he did it, but man, that cat could make a cassette sound like a Dolby 5.1. Little wonder he won five Grammy Awards, and was hired time and again by everybody from Paul McCartney to Oscar Peterson, Natalie Cole, and Duke Ellington. Plus, he has one of the best mustaches in show business.) Every time I finished listening to that record from beginning to end, I thought, *Now this is what I call drive-around music.*

Being that this was the first release on the Qwest label, Quincy wanted everything to be just right, from the sequencing to the packaging to the manner in which the singles were released. But Q's version of *just right* was different from the rest of the world's. When we went to present the album to the WEA bigwigs, he said, "Gentlemen, we're going to sit here and listen to this from beginning to end, then when it's done, I want you to assign a number to each of these songs, with ten being the song that has the most sales potential, and one being the one that has the least."

Now, most of these bigwigs were perfectly good businesspeople, but they didn't have ears. They wouldn't know a whole note from an eighth note, a major scale from a minor scale, or, in some particularly sad cases, a guitar from a drum.

The bigwigs seemed to enjoy it—at least they all stayed to listen to the whole thing—and they filled out their lists as Quincy had requested. He added up the numbers, then said, "Okay, I see you guys picked 'Love X Love' to be the first single. So we're going with 'Give Me the Night'."

Now, some bigwigs would've been insulted by such a blatant diss, but they loved and respected Quincy, in part because he's lovable and respectable, and in part because *Off the Wall* sold a few billion copies, so they were pretty sure he knew what he was talking about. And in this case, it became *real* apparent *real* fast that he *did* know of what he spoke: Within weeks of its release, the single hit number one on the *Billboard* soul chart, and the album hit number three on the pop chart.

I loved working with Quincy—we butt heads once in a while, so it wasn't always roses and puppy dogs, but he was an idea man who inspired folks to play at a gear they didn't even know they had. I would've worked with him anytime, anyplace, but he was a busy cat, so I didn't see him in the studio for another four years.

In 1984, Q scored a coup: He convinced Frank Sinatra to do an album for Qwest. Getting Sinatra was a huge deal—between 1970 and 1984, the cat had only recorded six albums—and Quincy wanted to do right by the Chairman, so, as was his MO, he hired an A-team of cats: We're talking, among others, Randy Brecker and Jon Faddis on trumpet; Frank Foster, Michael Brecker, and my old pal Ronnie Cuber on reeds; Lionel Hampton on vibes; Marcus Miller and Ray Brown on bass; and . . . *whew*, I could go on all day.

Quincy asked me aboard, and immediately after I agreed, I got nervous. I mean, this was Frank Sinatra, man, *Frank Sinatra*! He was the greatest, most prestigious pop artist of our time, the best of the best. He changed the music, he changed the movies, he changed the culture, and he was *connected*, so if you weren't nervous going into the studio with Frank, you had no soul. And no brain.

I tried to stay cool as I set up my gear and the engineer dialed in my levels. This wasn't a Benson record—this was a Sinatra record—and Q hired me to be a sideman, and that's exactly what I was going to be. I'd check out the chart, start playing when Q counted it off, do my thing, and get on out of there without causing a fuss.

As I'm warming up, in walks Frank. He strolled to the front of the studio, sat down on a stool, and gave the band a silent appraising once-over. After a minute that felt like an hour, he gestured in my direction and growled, "You."

I looked over my left shoulder, then my right—nobody was behind me. So I pointed at my chest and said quietly, "Me?"

Frank stood up and said, "Yeah. You. George Benson. You. What're you doing way the hell back there? Why aren't you up here next to me?"

My first thought: *Frank Sinatra knows who I am?*

My second thought: *Man, do you think I'm crazy enough to set up my gear next to you?*

My third thought: *I'd better get up there next to him before he decides to come back here and punch me out.*

After I hauled my guitar and stool all the way next to Frank, he looked me right in the eye and said, "Georgie, my friend, let's not even talk about your guitar. Everybody knows how great you are as a guitar player. Me, I love your voice."

I almost fell off of that stool. For years, critics all over the world wrote about how I shouldn't even be singing, and that one moment gave me the confidence to mentally fend off those nay-saying scribes. I knew that the next time a bad review hit me in the heart, all I'd need to do was flash back to that moment, and I'd be okay.

But it didn't end there.

As I left the studio that night, it dawned on me that I'd never seen a Frank Sinatra concert. My career moved so fast, and I was always so busy, that I rarely got to see *any* concerts, for that matter, but the fact that I hadn't experienced the Chairman live was a crying shame. That situation had to be alleviated as soon as possible, so when I found out he was doing a show at Carnegie Hall the following month, I scored a pair of tickets and cleared my calendar.

The night of the show, I could barely contain myself. I was going to see Frank Sinatra, with a full orchestra, at the greatest hall in the world! I was so excited about the whole thing that I wore the finest piece of clothing in my closet: a dynamic blue suede jacket designed by Bijan of Beverly Hills that cost me . . . well, let's just say it cost me a *lot*. My friend, Dr. Jeffrey Starr, and I took our seats, the show started, and it was everything I had hoped for. Frank's voice soared over the strings, and he had complete control of the stage and the audience. We were eating from the palm of his hand, and enjoying every bite.

About halfway through the show, he walked to the front of the stage and said, "I understand that one of my good friends is in the house tonight. Ladies and gentlemen, one of the most talented men I've ever met: His name is George Benson." As the crowd let out a collective *Waaaaaaaahhhhhhhhhhhhhhh,* Frank said, "Stand up, George!" Reluctantly, I lifted my backside off the seat a couple of inches and gave a little wave. Squinting his eyes, Frank continued, "George, I can't see you. Can somebody turn up the house lights, please?"

The lights popped on, and I mumbled to myself, "Man, is this really happening?" If you asked me six months ago, "Do you think

Frank Sinatra knows anything about you," I'd have given you a resounding no. But now, for the second time in two months, he not only acknowledged my presence but said nice things about me to boot. And from what I understand, Frank Sinatra didn't always have nice things to say.

After I sat down, the rest of the show was a blur. All I remember is that after the Chairman sang his final note, my fellow Sinatra lovers converged upon me, and I couldn't even get out of my aisle—heck, I couldn't even get out of my seat. I signed autographs and chatted with people for forty-five minutes. I can sometimes run out of energy when hanging out with fans—I like to pay everybody their proper attention, and that can sometimes wear you out—but I was in such a daze that I could've stayed there all night. That was the last time I ever saw Sinatra, but whenever I turn on the radio and hear those golden notes come from his golden throat, I'm transported right on back to those two short but life-altering encounters with Old Blue Eyes.

It was around then, the mid-1980s, that I really, truly found my groove—a groove that I've never lost, thank goodness—and by that I mean I'd developed enough confidence in myself, my voice, and my guitar playing that I was able to handle anything that anybody threw at me. You want me to do a big band album with the Count Basie Orchestra? *Bring it on! My pleasure!* You want me to join Tommy LiPuma at his new record label, GRP? *Heck, yeah!* You want me to continue circling the planet with my axe on my back and my beloved band by my side? *It would be my honor!*

Sure, there were moments that stood out, records that were exceptionally memorable, like *Givin' It Up*, with Al Jarreau—a meeting that was a long time coming. Al and I met in 1975, when we'd both signed with Warner Bros.; the promotional cats at the label put together a showcase so that their two new signees—us—could show what they could do, and that was an incredible day. Strictly by happenstance, we both played a version of Dave Brubeck's "Take

Five"—mine, instrumental, and his, vocal. The way he articulated those difficult lines at once blew me away and gave me something to aspire to. We clicked both personally and musically, and I think that deep down, we hoped we'd work together someday. I'm actually glad it took so long to arrive at that point, because by 2006, we were both at a time in our careers and our lives that a collaboration made perfect sense. It also made sense that we record the tune "Breezin'," with lyrics provided by Al.

Soon after the sessions were over, one of my friends asked me, "Man, isn't it risky that you would do something like that, mess with one of your best-known songs?"

I said, "No, absolutely not. See, 'Breezin'' is a classic, and a classic can't be diminished by taking an entirely different approach. The new version won't replace the old. Besides, look how many jazz cats have recorded 'Just Friends' since Charlie Parker: Sonny Stitt, Pat Martino, Frank Sinatra, Art Pepper, Ray Brown, Lee Morgan, Sarah Vaughan, Tal Farlow, Bob James. No matter how good any of those are—and some of them are quite good—they won't diminish what Bird did."

Backtracking, another one of my most cherished collaborations came in 1987, when I took to the studio with Earl Klugh for an album called—you guessed it—*Collaboration*. (That was only the second session I co-led, the first one being that CTI date with Joe Farrell.) Since I first met Earl back in Detroit, he went on to become one of the most highly respected, consistently selling cats in our scene, and, most importantly, he cranked out *baaaaad* record after *baaaaad* record (*Heart String, Night Songs, Life Stories, Hand Picked* . . . I could go on), earning himself Grammy after Grammy after Grammy. When I listen to Earl—and I listen a lot because I, like you, am a serious listener—I always marvel at the way somebody with a truly original voice approaches a song, and in his case, it goes even further beyond that, as Earl all but created a genre: acoustic classical-style jazz guitar. On *Collaboration*, he handled the acoustic, I handled the electric. Man, I'm proud of that album, and doubly proud of Earl.

When people think "George Benson," they don't necessarily think "McCoy Tyner," and I guess I can understand that: I'm probably best known for mellow things like "Breezin'" and "Nature Boy," and McCoy is probably best known for his five-plus years of smacking the piano around alongside John Coltrane. But lots of folks don't realize that I can amp it up and he can tone it down, and when we meet near the middle, *whoooo*, things happen. We've played big halls and small clubs, each and every one of which we've burnt to the ground. Our association has been documented on wax a couple of times, once on my album *Tenderly*, a straight-ahead ballads thing we cut in 1989, and another time on a burnin' collection of standards and slow stuff called *Round Midnight*. Some folks might think that because he can be so mean on piano that he's a mean person, but the fact is, McCoy Tyner is one of the sweetest cats the jazz world has ever produced, and he's among the finest pianists of our time.

The record business being the record business, not everything was roses. In 1993, after almost fifteen years and a dozen-plus albums, I left Warner Bros. They actually offered me a generous deal, but there were some real problems with how they handled my career, the primary one being that they wanted to pigeonhole me as an R&B artist. If you come to my shows, you know that my audiences are mixed, in terms of race, age, and musical loves, and it's possible that many of these folks don't listen to R&B radio, and it's even more possible that R&B radio won't play the jazz cuts. So I followed my old friend Tommy LiPuma to GRP, a mostly jazz label cofounded by the great keyboardist Dave Grusin. I was with them for almost ten years, and though we never quite took it to the moon *Breezin'*-style, we made some wonderful music—a handful of records that I'm proud to have in my discography.

In 2009, I cut my second record for Concord, an indie label out of California that, for the longest time, was known for its roster of straight-ahead jazz cats and kittens: Dave Brubeck, Rosemary Clooney, Tony Bennett, Marian McPartland, Woody Herman, Gene Harris, Benny Golson, Charlie Byrd, Mel Torme, and Cal Tjader, among many, many, many others. Some folks might think, *Wow, George Benson and Concord is not a logical match*, but that label is run by forward-thinking, open-minded music folks who want to release the best music they possibly can without being beholden to stylistic boundaries. The record with Al Jarreau was my first for Concord, and the second was *Songs and Stories*, the first record of mine in a long while that didn't include a single original composition of mine. See, I came to the conclusion that when you're making a record, the greatest thing you can do is come up with a great song. (That may sound simple, but if it were easy, everyone would do it.) One of the hallmarks of a great song is that people can listen to it, understand it, and relate to it right from bar one. So I thought it would be fun to try material from the best of the best: James Taylor, Bill Withers, Smokey Robinson, and my old friends Donny Hathaway and Rod Temperton. If nothing else, nobody could complain that we didn't load that thing up with *baaaaad* material.

In 2013, I came full circle with the album *Inspiration: A Tribute to Nat King Cole*. I heard Nat King Cole when I was a youngster, and I never forgot him. Like Wes Montgomery, he was one of the cats whose music flows through my heart and soul 24/7/365. I'd been performing Nat-oriented material in my set for years—"Nature Boy" being the most notable example—and it always felt *right*. It had been in the back of my head for years to do an album of his stuff, but I never felt ready. And then I was. And doing that album—a record on which I shared the studio with Idina Menzel, Wynton Marsalis, and the Henry Mancini Institute Orchestra—man, it was like coming home.

And thank goodness I had that opportunity, because finding a good home—a true home, a comfortable home, a musical home—is what all of us aspire to. Luckily for me, over the last five decades I'm always home, even when I'm on the road, because anywhere there's a guitar within arm's length—and when you're near me, there's *always* a guitar—that's the place I want to be.

Final Interlude

I Keep Going

I'm writing this in 2014, a year that, professionally speaking, was pretty much the same as 2004, which was pretty much the same as 1994, and so on all the way back till the 1950s. And I don't mean that in a bad way—it's more about the magic of consistency. See, I'm a creature of (jazz) habit: I practice every day, I gig a lot, and I record almost every year. I keep going.

I keep going because I need that challenge. Just because I've been doing it forever doesn't mean it's gotten any easier. I can't tell you how many times a fan or a journalist has said, "George, you have the best job in the world. It sounds like you barely have to work." That is far from the truth. See, I make things sound so simple that people think this lick or that run is easy . . . but it isn't. First I have to imagine it, then I have to figure out how to play it, then I have to decide when and where to use it, then I have to make it sound cool to the listener. These things take time; these things take thought. I take the time and I put in the thought because I have to.

I keep going because it's fun, and I dig sharing the fun. See, I like to enjoy my gigs—if I'm having fun, chances are considerably better that you'll have fun, too—and sometimes the shows seem loose, but trust me, nothing I do is haphazard. Besides, real life isn't always a jam session. Most jazz musicians speak the same language, and that language is second nature, but that doesn't mean we should take anything for granted. Sure, I could put together a group of heavy-weights, then, without a rehearsal, play a competent ninety-minute set with a repertoire consisting of eight long 12-bar bebop blues songs like Bird's "Now's the Time," because these heavies have played that tune—or similar tunes—thousands of times. But I want the Benson experience to be more substantial. I want to combine the spontaneity of a jam session with the well-oiled sound of a well-rehearsed band. Folks work hard for their money, and if they're going to spend it on me, I'm going to work hard in return.

I keep going because it's my duty to perpetuate the music that was started by folks like Duke Ellington. Duke was one of the cats who proved to the world that African Americans had plenty to offer, on every level: his intricate but beautiful compositions and arrange-ments; his incredible, influential piano playing; his skill of incorpo-rating sounds and vibes from all styles of jazz; his ability to connect with listeners of all ages and races. He helped people of every color look at African Americans with a different eye. Charlie Parker, while equally vital to the development of the music, was loved by the jazz world, but not at first. When he first came onto the scene, many jazz listeners, critics, and experts found Bird's uncompromising brand of bebop—the newfangled harmonies, the jagged rhythms, the warp-speed tempos, the jarring intervallic leaps—confusing and frighten-ing. But Duke Ellington proved that young African Americans might have something special to say, so folks stuck with Bird and eventually learned to love him. However, not everybody loves Bird; even today, his music scares some folks. A couple of years back, a woman took her father to one of my gigs. After telling me how much he enjoyed the show, he told me, "Mr. Benson, there was one guy from back in the day. He almost destroyed jazz. He had a name that sounded like an animal."

I said, "You mean Bird?"

He said, "That's it!"

"Charlie 'Yardbird' Parker."

"Yeah, that's the name. Yardbird. They said he was going to destroy jazz."

On the way back to the hotel, I thought about what the man said, what the man felt, what the man believed, and you know what? He was right. Charlie Parker improvised in a sophisticated manner that wasn't appreciated by every jazz ear at the time. He broke the mold, but he broke it in a way that enabled those who study his work to put it together in a new, beautiful manner, with a whole new identity, an identity that brought us to where we are now. And I think we're in a pretty good place.

Acknowledgments

My story is dedicated to my mom, Mrs. Erma Collier. Everybody loves their mom—it's a given. We all have a lot to be thankful for when it comes to our mothers, but when it comes to music, I have to give it all to my mom. Her love of music—present in everything she did—was passed on to me as a nursing baby. Even at mealtimes, she hummed while she chewed. She took me to see the films of the forties and fifties, which featured theme songs that were plastered into my brain and still reside there today. Although we didn't have a lot of money, she would spend her last nickel to make sure I was well cared for and had access to music and the musical instruments I begged her for. I love you, Mom.

I give thanks to the name Jehovah for the gifts he gave me to enhance the lives of so many people in a beautiful way.

Thank you to John Hammond, the greatest A&R man in jazz history; Creed Taylor, renaissance man; Herbie Hancock, Mr. Versatility; Ron Carter, Mr. Class himself; Freddie Hubbard, the powerhouse; Miles Davis, mentor; Quincy Jones, a song's best friend; Tommy LiPuma, master perfectionist; Al Schmitt, classy genius; Mo Ostin, problem neutralizer; Rudy Van Gelder, engineering wonder; and John Burk, visionary. Thanks also to Harry Tepper, Eugene Landy, Jimmy Boyd, Ken Fritz, and Dennis Turner for the invaluable advice and direction I received throughout the many different periods of my career.

Thanks to our terrific, patient, sharp-eyed, music-savvy editor, Ben Schafer, as well as Kevin Hanover, Kate Burke, Sean Maher, Justin Lovell, and Melody Negron, and to the entire team at Da Capo Press and the Perseus Books Group.

An extra-special thanks goes to Stephanie and Rick Gonzalez of Apropos Management/Marketing, who helped me tremendously with the creation of my life story and continue to help me with my career.

And last but not least, a heartfelt thank-you to Alan Goldsher, my trusty ghostwriter. Without Alan's hard work, deft writing touch, and deep-rooted knowledge of jazz history, this book would not have come to fruition.

Index

A&M Records, 131–133, 137, 167
"Ain't That Peculiar," 103
album(s): *Bad Benson*, 141, 146, 147;
Benson records, in New York City,
19–23; *Beyond the Blue Horizon*,
146; *Body Talk*, 141, 146; *Breezin'*,
164–173, 190; *Collaboration*,
204–205; *The Concert McDuff*,
71–72; cut with Brother Jack
McDuff, 69–70; *In Flight*, 174–175,
176; *The George Benson Cookbook*,
111–112; *Giblet Gravy*, 119–123;
Give Me the Night, 190–200; *Givin'
It Up*, 132, 203–204; *Good King
Bad*, 146, 199; *Hot Barbeque*, 76;
*Inspiration: A Tribute to Nat King
Cole*, 206; *It's Uptown with the
George Benson Quartet*, 103;
judging, 103–104; *Little Georgie
Benson: The Kid from Gilmore Alley*,
21–23; *Live at the Front Room*,
69–70; *Livin' Inside Your Love*, 190;
*The New Boss Guitar of George
Benson*, 79–80; *The Other Side of
Abbey Road*, 132–133; recording,
164–165, 186; *Round Midnight*, 205;
Shape of Things to Come, 132; *Silk
and Soul*, 76; *Songs and Stories*, 206;
Tenderly, 205; *Weekend in L.A.*,
182–186, 190; *White Rabbit*, 139,
141–142, 146, 188
Alexander, Monty, 108
Ali, Muhammad, 177–181
All Stars, 42–43
Alpert, Herb, 131–132
Altairs: Benson leaves, 42; creation of,
29, 32–33; effect of, on Benson's
education, 40–41; guitar player for,
34–36; musical growth through,
38–39; success of, 33–34
Ammons, Gene (Jug), 156–157
amplifier, John McLaughlin blows out,
129–130
"Angel Eyes," 166
antifreeze, 51–52
Arista Records, 179–180
Armstrong, Louis, 116, 155
art teacher, 40–41
Arthur Godfrey Show, The, 20
awards, 139

Babbitt, Bob, 2
Bad Benson, 141, 146, 147
Bags Meets Wes! (Montgomery), 82
Bailey, Donald, 44
Baker's Keyboard Lounge, 186–187
Banks, Stanley, 145, 172
Barkan, Todd, 161